C000253985

HEADING FOR HEAVEN

HEADING
FOR
HEAVEN

J.C.RYLE

 EVANGELICAL PRESS

EP BOOKS
Faverdale North, Darlington, DL3 0PH, England

web: http://www.epbooks.org

e-mail: sales@epbooks.org

EP BOOKS USA
P. O. Box 614, Carlisle, PA 17013, USA

www.epbooks.us

e-mail: usasales@epbooks.org

First published in this format 1987
Reprinted 2009

This book is a selection of chapters from *The Christian race*, originally published by Evangelical Press in 1978 under the title *The true Christian*.

British Library Cataloguing in Publication Data available

ISBN-13 978-0-85234-710-2

Printed in Great Britain by Athenaeum Press Ltd, Gateshead.

Contents

1.
One way

1.
One way

" Enoch walked with God, and he was not : for God took him."
Genesis 5:24

YOU all wish to go to heaven. I know it. I am fully persuaded of it ; I am certain of it. There is not one of you, however false may be his views of what he must believe and what he must do, however unscriptural the ground of his hope, however worldly-minded he may be during the week, however careless when he gets outside that door—there is not one of you, I say, who does not wish to go to heaven. But I do sadly fear that many of you, without a mighty change, will never get there. You would like the crown, but you do not like the cross ; you would like the glory, but not the grace ; the happiness, but not the holiness ; the peace, but not the truth ; the victory, but not the fight ; the reward, but not the labour ; you would like the harvest, but not the ploughing ; you would like the reaping, but not the sowing ; and so I fear that many of you will never get to heaven.

Well, you may say, these are sharp words, this is hard measure ; but we should like to know what sort of people they are who will be saved. I shall give you a short and very general answer. They who have the same faith as those holy men whose names are recorded in the Bible—they who walk in that same

narrow path which all the saints of God have trodden
—such persons and such only shall have eternal life
and never enter into condemnation.

Indeed, beloved, there is but one way to heaven;
and in this way every redeemed soul that is now in
Paradise has walked. This is the way you must yourselves be content to follow; and if you are really
wise, if you really love life, as you profess to do, you
will take every opportunity of examining the characters
of those who have gone before you, you will mark
the principles on which they acted, you will note the
end they had in view, you will try to profit by their
experience, you will follow them so far as they followed
Christ.

Now, I purpose this morning to speak to you about
the history of Enoch, who was one of the first among
those who by faith and patience have inherited the
promises; and I shall divide what I have to say upon
the subject into four parts.

I. What was the character of the age in which he
lived?

II. What was his own character?

III. What was the leading motive or principle which
influenced him?

IV. What was his end?

God grant that you may all be stirred up to a
diligent inquiry into your own state; may many of you,
hearing how Enoch walked with God, be led to pray,
"Lord, I would walk with Thee (I have sinned, but I
repent in dust and ashes), Lord Jesus, I would be Thine,
create in me a clean heart, guide me with Thy counsel,
and afterward bring me unto glory."

I. Now, respecting the age when Enoch lived we
know little, but that little is very bad. He was the
seventh from Adam, and lived in the time before the

flood. In those days, we are told, the earth was corrupt before God, and filled with violence. Every sort of wickedness seems to have prevailed ; men walked after the vile lusts of their hearts, and did that which appeared good to them without fear and without shame. The children of Cain, after he murdered Abel, as far as we can learn, made no attempt whatever to keep God in their thoughts,—like the prodigal son, they went afar off from Him and gave themselves up to worldly employments, as if they would keep the Lord out of their minds as much as possible. They got a name as founders of cities, like men who looked upon this earth as their home, and set all their affection on things below and had no desire after the new Jerusalem above, the city of the Lord God and of the Lamb. They became famous and skilful in all the works of this life : one was called the father of shepherds, and another the father of musicians ; but we read of none that was a father of faithful lambs in Christ's flock, of none that was a father of children who made God's statutes their song in the house of their pilgrimage. And another was a teacher of artificers in brass and iron ; but we do not hear of any who taught the good knowledge of the Lord. In short, they were all clever in finding out how to be rich and how to be merry and how to be powerful ; but they were not wise unto salvation, there was nothing of God and His fear and His service among them.

Such were the children of Cain ; and they seem to have been such pleasant company, so little disposed to trouble other people by talking about the soul and heaven and hell, that nearly everybody took after them, and the world was tainted and infected with their manners ; insomuch that the few who still clung to the true God became separated from the rest by a line of distinction : they began to be called by the name of the Lord.

But even this separation did not last long. We are next told, that they who professed to be the sons of God began to think there was no harm in marrying persons who cared nothing about religion ; they chose wives who were unbelievers,—beautiful and agreeable, no doubt, but still enemies of God,—and (as it has almost always proved when a Christian has been united to one that is not a Christian), the bad soon corrupted the good, or else the good did not convert the bad, and the families that were born of these unions proved earthly, sensual, and devilish, and in a short time the whole world was full of sin.

Consider, beloved, what a fearful proof you have here of the natural bent of man's heart towards wickedness ! They had the recollection of God's anger against transgression fresh upon their minds ; they had Paradise before their eyes, they had the angels of God keeping the way of the tree of life with flaming swords ; and yet, in spite of all this, they sinned with a high hand. They went on much as the world likes to do now : they ate, they drank, they planted, they builded, they bought, they sold, they made light of warnings. " What have we do with the Lord ? " they thought ; " let us enjoy ourselves while we can." But God will not be mocked, and though He bore with them long and exhorted them by His servants, He dealt with them at last according to their works ; and just as He will one day send the fire upon this earth, so did He send the waters of the deep : the flood came and cut them off in the middle of their revellings, and drowned the whole world excepting eight persons.

Such was the character of the men before the flood ; and in the middle of this age of wickedness Enoch

lived, and Enoch walked with God. There were no
Bibles then, no prayer-books, no religious tracts, no
churches, no ministers, no sacraments: Christ had never
been seen; the way of salvation had never been clearly
made known; the gospel was only seen dimly in the
distance; it was not fashionable to think about religion,
it was not fashionable to worship God at all, there
was nothing to encourage people to make a profession.
Yet in the middle of this wicked and adulterous generation this saint of the Most High did live; Enoch walked
with God. It is almost impossible to imagine a more
splendid proof of what grace can do for a weak, sinful
man than is to be found in these words; in the world
before the flood " Enoch walked with God."

II. I promised in the second place to tell you something about Enoch's character. You have heard he
walked with God, and you know, perhaps, it is an
expression of great praise; but I may not leave you
here without trying to give you a clear notion of its
meaning. People often get a habit of using words without exactly knowing what they mean, and a very bad
habit it is. Now, I say that this walking with God has
many different senses; it is an expression full of matter.

A man that walks with God is one of *God's friends.*
That unhappy enmity and dislike which men naturally
feel towards their Maker has been removed; he feels
perfectly reconciled and at peace. How indeed can
two walk together except they be agreed? He does
not hide himself from the Lord, like Adam in the
trees of the garden, but he seeks to be in constant
communion with Him; he is not as many who are
uncomfortable at the idea of being alone with God
for he is never perfectly happy excepting in His company; he feels that he cannot be too much with Him,
because he desires to be of the same mind, to think

like Him, to act like Him, to be conformed to His image.
Such a one was Enoch.

Again, he that walks with God is one of *God's dear
children.* He looks upon Him as his Father, and as
such he loves Him, he reveres Him, he rejoices in Him,
he trusts Him in everything. He makes it his constant
study to please Him, and whenever he has offended,
he sorrows over his offence with a true childlike sorrow.
He thinks that God knows better than himself what
is good for him, and so in everything that happens—
sickness or health, sorrow or joy, riches or poverty—he
says to himself, " It is well: my Father sends this."
Such a one was Enoch.

Again, he that walks with God is one of *God's
witnesses.* He never hesitates to stand forward on
the Lord's side. He is not content with giving his
own heart to God, but he is also ready and willing
to bear his testimony in public on behalf of the cause
of righteousness and truth. He is not ashamed to
let men know whose servant he is; he will not be
turned aside from raising his voice against sin for fear
of giving offence. Such a one was Enoch. His lot
was cast in evil days; but did he join the multitude?
Did he walk in the way of sinners? Did he hold his
peace and say, I can do nothing? Far from it! He
thought not what his neighbours liked, but what his
Lord required. He sought not to please the world,
but to please God; and therefore, living in the midst
of sin and corruption, he was separate from it. He
was a witness against it; he was as the salt of the
earth; he was as a light shining in a dark place.

Ay, and he was a plain speaker, too. He made
no excuse about youth and temptation; he did not
let men go to hell for fear of being thought uncharitable, but he told them openly of their danger; and

when they were living wickedly and carelessly, as if there was no God and no devil, he said, as the apostle Jude relates, "The Lord cometh with ten thousand of His saints, to execute judgment upon all, and to convince all that are ungodly of their ungodly deeds." No doubt he was thought a troubler of the people, and a disagreeable man ; but he was a witness, and so he declared continually : "The Lord cometh"; whether ye will hear or whether ye will forbear, there shall be a day of account, sin shall not always go unpunished—repent, for the Lord cometh. This was the burden of his testimony. He walked with God, and so he was a faithful witness.

But I say further, to walk with God is to walk in *God's ways*, to follow the laws He has given for our guidance, to look on His precepts as our rule and our counsellor, to esteem all His commandments concerning all things to be right ; to fear turning aside from the narrow path He has set before us for one single instant ; to go straightforward, though all things seem against us, remembering the word on which He has caused us to hope.

And to walk with God is to walk in the light of God's countenance ; to live as men who remember that all things are naked and opened unto the eyes of Him with whom we have to do, that the darkness is no darkness with Him, and remembering this, to aim at never thinking or saying or doing anything we should be ashamed of in the presence of the great Searcher of hearts.

And to walk with God is to walk after the Spirit— to look to the Holy Ghost as our Teacher, to lean on Him for strength, to put no confidence in the flesh, to set our affections on things above, to wean them from things on earth, to be spiritually-minded.

But truly, beloved, I might keep you here all day, and yet the half would not be told of the things which are contained in walking with God. To walk with God is to walk humbly confessing ourselves unworthy of the least of all His mercies, acknowledging that we have no power of ourselves to help ourselves, that we are constantly coming short and backsliding, that we are unprofitable servants, and without His grace are sure to fall. It is to walk circumspectly, bearing in mind our besetting sins and temptations, and avoiding all places and companies and employments in which we are likely to be assailed by them. It is to walk in love towards all, both God and man, full of the mind that is in our heavenly Father, kind and affectionate and gentle to every one, yea, even to the unthankful and the evil. To walk with God is to serve Him as a habit, continually; we are not to walk with Him on a Sunday and forget Him on a weekday; we are not to walk with Him in public but not in private; we are not to walk with Him before ministers and good men only, but in our own families and before our own household.

And lastly, to walk with God is to be always going forward, always pressing on, never standing still and flattering ourselves that we are the men and have borne much fruit; but to grow in grace, to go on from strength to strength, to forget the things behind, and if by grace we have attained unto anything, to abound yet more and more.

Beloved, this is a very faint picture of a walk with God, but time will not allow me to draw another stroke. This was some part of Enoch's character; this was in some degree the meaning of the record God has given us about him.

Oh, it is a simple but a weighty record! No doubt

there were many great and many wise and many noble
in those days; but all we know of them is that they
lived and they died and they begat sons and daughters.
Of Enoch only is it written that he walked with God.
Oh, this walk with God, beloved! It is the only talent
which will never fail us, the only treasure which will
prove eternal, the only character which will serve us
beyond the grave; and in the day when names and
titles and honours shall sink to nothing, and all shall
stand upon a level, the poorest and the humblest in
the land shall be more highly honoured than the mighty
and the rich, if he has walked with God and they have
not; the first shall be last and the last first.

Comfort ye, comfort ye, all that belong to Christ's
little flock; comfort ye, all that are thinking first about
your souls; others may live in courts and palaces and
have the praise of this world, but of you it shall be
written in the books of heaven, "They walked with
God"; the King of kings and Lord of lords was their
Shepherd, their Guide, their Companion, their familiar
Friend, and your joy shall no man take away.

III. I must now say a few words about Enoch's
motive. He walked with God; and you will ask me,
"What was the secret cause of it, what was the hidden
spring and principle which influenced him, that we may
go forth and do likewise?" Beloved, God has told us
plainly in the Epistle to the Hebrews—it was faith.
Faith was the seed which bore such goodly fruit; faith
was the root of his holiness and decision on the Lord's
side—faith without which there has never been any
salvation, faith without which not one of you will ever
enter into the kinglom of heaven.

Now this faith is no mystery; it is neither more nor
less than a thorough belief of the heart.

Enoch believed that as a child of Adam he was

himself born a sinner and deserving of nothing but
wrath and condemnation ; he believed that his first
parents had forfeited all right to eternal life, and that
he as one of their descendants had inherited a heart
deceitful above all things and desperately wicked.   He
did not merely look upon himself as naturally very
thoughtless and liable to be led away by bad company,
and the like, as many of you are content to do, but
he went further, he looked within and laid the blame
on the old Adam, the corrupt fountain of his own heart ;
he really believed himself to be a miserable sinner.

But Enoch believed that God had graciously provided
a way of salvation, that He had appointed a great
Redeemer to bear our sins and carry our transgressions
and bruise the serpent's head.   He saw clearly that
without this he had not the slightest chance of being
saved, whatever he might do ; he looked far forward,
and in his mind's eye he saw a long way off the Messiah
that was yet to come to pay the ransom of the world,
and he built all his hopes on Him.   Enoch believed
in the Lord Jesus Christ.

And Enoch believed that God was a God of perfect
holiness, " of purer eyes than to behold iniquity."   He
never held with those who said, " You are righteous
overmuch, the Lord will not be so very particular, we
need not be so very strict, men cannot be always keeping watch over themselves ; " for he trembled at the
thought of allowing himself in any shadow of impurity
or unrighteousness ; and though he never dreamed of
setting up his own works as anything worth, though
he rejoiced in the hope of salvation by free grace, still
he believed that he who walks with God and would
have eternal life must be holy even as He is holy.

And Enoch believed that God would one day come
to judge the world and give to all men according to

their works. Though iniquity abounded and the love of many waxed cold, and all things seemed to go on as if God took no notice of this earth, he still believed the Lord would come to take account in such an hour as no one expected Him ; in faith he saw the judgment close at hand, and he walked with God as one waiting for it. He lived as if he felt this was not his rest ; he looked beyond the things which are seen to that abiding city which remaineth for the people of God ; by faith he saw that heaven was his only home and in the Lord's presence alone was fulness of joy. Such was the ruling principle which possessed this holy man of old. Oh that you would pray earnestly for a like precious faith ! Without it you will never walk in Enoch's way, and so you will never come to Enoch's end.

IV. And this leads me, in the last place, to speak about Enoch's end. We are simply informed in the text that " He was not, for God took him." The interpretation of this is, that God was pleased to interfere in a special manner on His servant's behalf, and so He suddenly removed him from this world without the pains of death, and took him to that blessed place where all the saints are waiting in joyful expectation for the end of all things, where sin and pain and sorrow are no more.

And this, no doubt, was done for several reasons. It was done to convince a hard-hearted, unbelieving world that God does observe the lives of men and will honour those who honour Him. It was done to show every living soul that Satan had not won a complete victory when he deceived Eve ; that men may yet get to heaven by the way of faith, and although in Adam all die, still in Christ all may be made alive. Yes, beloved, Enoch walked with God, and so God took him. Here was a splendid and a comforting assurance that the Lord's eye is upon all His children, that there is a heaven and a life to come, that there is a reward for the righteous, though men may laugh at them, and their walk is not fashionable, and their way is spoken against and their seriousness is despised. Oh, cast not away your confidence, ye that walk with God : it is but a little season and He that shall come will come and take you to an everlasting rest.

And now, beloved, I do beseech you all, if you care about your souls,—if you really desire to go to heaven, —if you really have the slightest wish to die in peace, and rise in glory, and join the company of the just,— I do beseech you ask yourselves the question, " Am I walking with God ? am I in that way which Enoch and all the saints have walked in ? " How many among you have one grain of that living faith which guided this holy man's feet into the way of peace ?

Would you have me suppose they are walking with God who live in any known sin which the Bible condemns ? Are they walking with God who regard Him and His service in the second place and the care of this world's matters in the first ? Are they who never think, and say to each other " Never mind this anxiety—I dare say we shall be right at last " ? Are they who neglect any means of grace which God has placed within their reach, or let the most trifling excuse prevent their using it ? Are they who profess to know the Lord and believe in Jesus, but do not make Jesus their example ? Oh ! no, no ! It is impossible ; all such must be walking away from God ; day after day they get farther from Him, and at last, unless they turn, they will walk into hell.

And when I see men going towards this place of torment—for all must be who are not walking with

God—when I see the loving and tender-hearted Lord
Jesus holding out His hands and saying, " Come unto
me : why will ye die ? I can and will cleanse you from
all sin ! "—when I see all this, and find you cold and
undecided, and flattering yourselves you are in a middle
path and tolerably safe, I must cry aloud and spare
not, and run the risk of being thought uncharitable, if
by any means I may awaken you and deliver you from
the power of Satan and guide you unto Christ. Oh
that your hearts may be stirred within you, that you
may never rest till you are in Enoch's way and have
some portion of Enoch's faith !

Think not to put off the question by saying these
things cannot be true. Go to your Bibles and see what
they testify. They that are utterly deceived and blind
may tell you that punishment is not eternal, and hell
is a delusion, and the devil a lie ; but they will find to
their cost they are all true, most fearfully true, and so
long as you attend the worship of the Church of
England, which only appeals to Scripture, you must
not expect to hear of any other way than that which
Enoch took.

Think not to say, " We cannot walk with God : we
mean well in church, but when we get outside the
world lays hold upon us, and acquaintances and evil
company turn us aside." Oh, be honest with yourselves !
This is as much as saying " If all the world be religious
we will be religious too, and not till then " ; in the meanwhile you do not like to be singular, you cannot make
up your minds to be in earnest, you think I may be
mistaken, you will go with the stream, you will walk
according to the course of this world. But look at
Enoch : his heart was naturally like yours ; the same
grace which strengthened him can strengthen you,—the
Lord's hand is not shortened ; by grace he walked with

God three hundred years, and surely you may trust the power of God will keep you also through faith unto salvation for threescore years and ten. But know that if you cannot be saints on earth you never can be saints in heaven.

Think not I am shutting you up without hope. What though it be true that few are saved and the way is narrow?—there is nothing to prevent any of you entering it, except your own unwillingness, your own unbelieving hearts, your own indifference. Oh, begin to walk as Enoch did! Come to the Lord Jesus Christ! He that cometh to Him shall never hunger, he that believeth on Him shall never thirst: though your past life may have been that of Esau or Manasseh or Judas or Mary Magdalen, come to Him repenting of everything, and He will never cast you out. Take with you words; and say, " Lord Jesus, I have sinned; I do repent, I put all my trust in thee: Lord receive me, Lord increase my faith," and then the word of God is my warrant for saying He shall give you His Holy Spirit, and you shall walk with Him and before Him and after Him, and rest with Him.

Are you old?—then walk with God; and be in haste: your next step may be in hell; thank the Lord you are not there yet. You have but a short time; you hang by a slender thread; Jordan is before you, and you will never cross in safety unless the ark is with you, and the ark is only with those who walk with God.

Are you young?—then walk with God, and be in haste. Do not put it off a single day. Young people die as well as old. Young people have precious souls to save as well as others. The devil, who rejoices to see so many of you neglecting private prayers and private reading of the Bible, has an especial eye to you: he knows if he can only prevent you thinking while you are young, he has a better chance of making you his own forever.

O let it not be written of you in the books of God that on this Sabbath day you came together not for the better but for the worse ; you were invited to walk with God, and would not : let it not be in vain you have heard this history of one of the Lord's elect ; but cast aside your old habits, arise to newness of life, even as the face of the fair country around you is renewed at this season of the year ; and be ye followers of Enoch even as he followed God.

Remember, all of you, the prophecy he spake : " the Lord cometh, to execute judgment." This earth, lovely and fair and shining as it seems, shall be burned up ; but your soul shall live for ever, either in heaven or in hell : this very Church shall crumble into dust, but they that sleep around it shall rise again, bone shall come together unto bone, and all stand before the throne and be judged according to their lives. The Lord grant you may all find mercy in that day ; but if you would find it, you must walk with God, and then indeed you shall live by faith and sleep in Jesus and have your portion with the spirits of just men made perfect.

2.
Running the race

2.
Running the race

" Seeing we also are compassed about with so great a cloud of witnesses, let us lay aside every weight, and the sin which doth so easily beset us, and let us run with patience the race that is set before us, looking unto Jesus the author and finisher of our faith." *Hebrews 12:1,2*

BELOVED, I have lately spoken to you much about the character and experience of true believers in the Lord Jesus Christ, the men who are sowing for everlasting life.

Before, however, we continue this inquiry, I wish to warn you against forgetting the sure foundation ; I wish to caution you most strongly against losing sight of the root of the whole matter—a simple faith in the Lord Jesus Christ. You must not stumble at the outset by supposing I want you to set up a righteousness of your own. Some think their own endeavours after holiness are to make up their title to salvation ; some think that when they come to Christ, their sins past alone are forgiven, and for the time to come they must depend upon themselves. Alas! there always have been mistakes upon this point : men toil and labour after peace with God as if their own exertions would give them a right to lay hold on Christ, and when they find themselves far short of the Bible standard they mourn and grieve and will not be comforted ; and all because they will not see that in the matter of forgiveness, in the matter of justification in the sight of God, it is not doing which is required, but believing ; it is not working, but trusting ; it is not perfect obedience, but humble faith.   Now, once for all, let us understand, that all who have really fled for mercy to the Lord Jesus Christ are, as Paul assures the Colossians, complete in Him !   In themselves they may be poor shortcoming sinners, but seeing they have laid hold on Christ, God looks upon them as complete— completely pardoned, completely righteous, completely pure—no jot or tittle of condemnation can be laid to their charge.

They have nothing more to do with the law as a covenant of works, as a condition they must fulfil or die : the Lord does not say, " Be perfect and then you shall live," but " Christ has given you life, and for His sake strive to be perfect."   But you will ask me, " Why do they hunger and thirst so much after holiness, since all their debt has been paid ? "   I answer, They work for love's sake—for gratitude ; they do not work and strive after holiness in order that they may be forgiven, but because they are forgiven already, chosen and sealed and saved and redeemed and bought with a price, and they cannot help desiring to glorify Him with their bodies and spirits who loved them and gave Himself for them.   They thirst after holiness because their Father loves holiness ; they thirst after purity because their Master loves purity ; they strive to be like Jesus because they hope to be one day for ever with Him.

But seeing they have many a difficulty in doing the things that they would, and are continually warring with the world, the flesh, and the devil, and sometimes are so ready to faint that they doubt whether they really are of Christ's family or not,—seeing these things are so, I have tried to give you a faint outline of their experience on late occasions, and I purpose this afternoon to lay before you shortly the advice which the apostle gives them in my text.

Now, I say that the text contains five points :

I. We have all a race to run.

II. Many have gone before us.

III. We must lay aside every weight.

IV. We must run with patience.

V. We must be continually looking unto Jesus. The Lord pour down His Spirit upon each of you, and bow the hearts of all here present, as the heart of one man, that you may seek the Lord while there is yet time, and set your faces towards Jerusalem, and not die the death of the faithless and unbelieving.

I. First, then, we have a *race to run*. By this you are not to understand that our own right arm and our own strength can ever open for us the gates of everlasting life, and win us a place in heaven. Far from it : that is all of grace—it is another question. It simply means that all who take up the cross and follow Christ must make up their minds to meet with many a difficulty, they must calculate on labour and toil and trouble, they have a mighty work to do, and there is need for all their attention. Without there will be fightings, within there will be fears ; there will be snares to be avoided, and temptations to be resisted ; there will be your own treacherous hearts, often cold and dead and dry and dull ; there will be friends who will give you unscriptural advice, and relations who will even war against your soul ; in short, there will be stumbling-blocks on every side, there will be occasion for all your diligence and watchfulness and godly jealousy and prayer,—you will soon find that to be a real Christian is no light matter.

Oh what a condemnation there is here for all those easy-going persons who seem to think they may pass their time as they please, and yet be numbered with the saints in glory everlasting! Are those who show less earnestness about their souls than about their earthly amusements, and those who have much to tell you about this world's business but nothing about heaven, and those who think nothing of neglecting the commonest helps towards Zion, and count it much to give religion a few Sunday thoughts,—are these men running the Christian race, and straining every nerve after the prize? I leave the answer with yourselves: judge ye what I say.

And those who profess to have entered the course, and yet find time to rest by the wayside and trifle with temptation, and find fault with the anxiety of others,—and those who stop to take breath and boast of their attainments, and look behind them,—are such running the race set before them as if it was a matter of life and death? Oh no! They may get the name of Christians, but they are not so running that they shall obtain. But they who are taught and called of God may soon be distinguished from the sleeping children of this world. These have no leisure for vain amusements; their eyes are fixed and their thoughts are engaged upon the narrow path they have to tread and the crown they hope to receive; they have counted the cost, and come out from the world; and their only wish is that they may finish their course with joy.

II. The second thing you may learn from the text is this: " Many have gone before us; we are encompassed with a great cloud of *witnesses*." The witnesses here spoken of are those patriarchs and prophets who are mentioned in the eleventh chapter, and the apostle calls upon us to remember them and their troubles and take courage. Are we frail earthen vessels? so were they. Are we weak and encompassed with infirmities? so were they. Are we exposed to temptation and burdened with this body of corruption? so were they. Are we afflicted? so were they. Are we alone in our generation, the scorn of all our neighbours? so were they. Have we trials of cruel mockings? so had they. What can we possibly be called upon to suffer which they have not endured? What consolations did they receive which we may not enjoy? You may talk of your cares and business and families, but their portion was just like yours; they were men of like passions; they did not neglect business, and yet they gave their hearts to God. They show the race can always be run by those who have the will. Yes, they were all flesh and blood like ourselves, and yet by grace they became new creatures; and so by faith they "obtained a good report;" by faith they confessed themselves strangers and pilgrims on the earth; through faith they "subdued kingdoms, wrought righteousness, obtained promises, stopped the mouths of lions, quenched the violence of fire, escaped the edge of the sword, out of weakness were made strong, waxed valiant in fight, turned to flight the armies of the aliens: women received their dead raised to life again; and others were tortured not accepting deliverance, that they might obtain a better resurrection; and others had trial of bonds and imprisonment: they were stoned, they were sawn asunder, were tempted, were slain with the sword; they wandered about in sheepskins and goatskins, being destitute, afflicted, tormented." But grace exceedingly abounded, and all fought a good fight and finished their course and kept the faith, and to the God of gods appeared every one of them in Zion. Take courage, fainting Christians: you are encompassed with a great cloud of witnesses; the race that you are running has been run by millions before; you think that no one ever had

such trials as yourself, but every step that you are
journeying has been safely trod by others ; the valley
of the shadow of death has been securely passed by a
cloud of trembling, doubting ones like yourself; they
had their fears and anxieties, like you, but they were
not cast away ; the world, the flesh and the devil can
never overwhelm the weakest woman who will set her
face towards God ; these millions journeyed on in
bitterness and tears like your own, and yet not one
did perish—they all reached home.

III. The third point to be considered is the apostle's
advice, to "lay aside every weight." By this he means
that we must give up everything which is *really hurtful
to our souls*. We must act like men who throw off
all their long and flowing garments, as an encumbrance,
when about to try their speed in running. We must
cast away everything which hinders us upon our road
towards heaven—the lust of the flesh, the lust of the
eye, and the pride of life ; the love of riches, pleasures,
and honours, the spirit of lukewarmness and carelessness
and indifference about the things of God, all must be
rooted out and forsaken if we are anxious for the prize.
We must mortify the deeds of the body, we must crucify
our affection for this world ; we must look well to our
habits and inclinations and employments, and if we
find anything coming in as a stumbling-block between
ourselves and salvation, we must be ready to lay it
aside as if it were a millstone about our necks, although
it cost us as much pain as cutting off a hand or plucking
out a right eye. Away with everything which keeps
us back ; our feet are slow at the very best, we have
a long course to run, we cannot afford to carry weight,
if we are really contending for everlasting life.

But above all we must take heed that we lay aside
the sin which doth most easily beset us, the sin which

from our age, or habit, or taste, or disposition, or feelings, possesses the greatest power over us. I know of two which are always at our elbows, two sins which try the most advanced Christians even to the end, and these are pride and unbelief—pride in our own difference from others, pride in our reputation as Christians, pride in our spiritual attainments: unbelief about our own sinfulness, unbelief about God's wisdom, unbelief about God's mercy. Oh, they are heavy burdens, and sorely do they keep us back, and few really know they are carrying them, and few indeed are those who will not discover them at the very bottom of the chamber of their hearts, waiting an opportunity to come out.

But there are particular besetting sins, of which each separate Christian can alone furnish an account; each single one of us has some weak point, each one has got a thin, shaking spot in his wall of defence against the devil, each one has a traitor in his camp ready to open the gates to Satan, and he that is wise will never rest until he has discovered where this weak point is. This is that special sin which you are here exhorted to watch against, to overcome, to cast forth, to spare no means in keeping it under and bringing it into subjection, that it may not entangle you in your race towards Zion. One man is beset with lust, another with a love of drinking, another with evil temper, another with malice, another with covetousness, another with worldly-mindedness, another with idleness; but each of us has got about him some besetting infirmity, which is able to hinder him far more than others, and with which he must keep an unceasing warfare, or else he will never so run as to obtain the prize. *Oh these bitter besetting sins!* How many have fallen in their full course, and given occasion to God's enemies to blaspheme, from thinking lightly of them, from not continually guarding against them, from a vain notion that they were altogether cut off!—they have been over-confident and presumptuous; they have said "We are the temple of the Lord, and we cannot greatly stumble," and they have forgotten that hidden root, that branch of the old Adam; and so day after day, little by little, shoot after shoot, it grew, it strengthened, it filled their heart, it blighted their few graces; and suddenly, without time to think, they have slipped and fallen headlong in the race, and now they are hurrying down stream amidst that miserable party, the backsliders, and who can tell what their end may be? But what was the simple cause? They disregarded some besetting sin. Go, child of God, and search the chamber of thine imagination: see whether thou canst find there some seed of evil, some darling thing which thou hast tenderly spared hitherto, because it was a little one; away with it—there must be no mercy, no compromise; no reserve: it must be laid aside, plucked up, torn up by the roots, or it will one day trip thee up, and prevent thee running thy race towards Zion. The gates of heaven are broad enough to receive the worst of sinners, but too narrow to admit the smallest grain of unforsaken sin.

IV. The fourth point to be noticed in the text is the frame of mind in which we are to run: "let us run with *patience*." I take this patience to mean that meek, contented spirit, which is the child of real living faith, which flows from a confidence that all things are working together for our good. Oh, it is a most necessary and useful grace! There are so many crosses to be borne when we have entered the course, so many disappointments and trials and fatigues, that, except we are enabled to possess our souls in patience, we shall never persevere unto the end. But we must not turn back to Egypt, because some bring up an evil report of the promised land ; we must not faint because the journey is long and the way lies through a wilderness, we must press forward without flagging, not murmuring when we are chastened, but saying, with Eli, " It is the Lord: let Him do that which seemeth Him good." Look at Moses, in Hebrews xi.: "When he was come to years, he refused to be called the son of Pharaoh's daughter ; choosing rather to suffer affliction with the people of God, than to enjoy the pleasures of sin for a season ; esteeming the reproach of Christ greater riches than the treasures of Egypt : for he had respect unto the recompence of the reward ; he endured as seeing Him who is invisible." Look at Job, when God permitted Satan to afflict him: "Naked," he says, " came I out of my mother's womb, and naked shall I return thither : the Lord gave, and the Lord hath taken away ; blessed be the name of the Lord." " What ? shall we receive good at the hand of God, and shall we not receive evil ?" Look at David, the man after God's own heart, how many waves of trouble passed over that honoured head ; how many years he fled from the hand of Saul, how much tribulation did he suffer from his own family ; and hear what he says when he is fleeing from his own son Absalom, and a certain Benjamite came forth and cursed him. " Behold, my son, which came forth of my bowels, seeketh my life : how much more may this Benjamite do it ? Let him alone, and let him curse ; for the Lord hath bidden him. It may be that the Lord will look on mine affliction, and that the Lord will requite me good for his cursing this day." Mark too, as you read his Psalms, how often you come on that expression, " waiting upon God": it seems as if he thought it the highest grace a Christian can attain to.

Look lastly at your blessed Lord Himself. St. Peter says, " He left us an example, that we should walk in His steps: who did no sin, neither was guile found in His mouth: who when He was reviled, reviled not again; when He suffered, He threatened not; but committed Himself to Him that judgeth right-eously." Paul says: " For consider Him that endured such contradiction of sinners against Himself, lest ye be wearied and faint in your minds. Ye have not yet resisted unto blood, striving against sin. And ye have forgotten the exhortation which speaketh unto you as unto children, My son, despise not thou the chastening, of the Lord, nor faint when thou art rebuked of Him: for whom the Lord loveth He chasteneth, and scourgeth every son whom He re-ceiveth." O yes, beloved, we must run with patience, or we shall never obtain. There may be many things we cannot understand, much that the flesh could perhaps wish otherwise; but let us endure unto the end, and all shall be made clear, and God's arrange-ments shall be proved best. Think not to have your reward on earth, do not draw back because your good things are all yet to come: to-day is the cross, but to-morrow is the crown; to-day is the labour, to-morrow is the wages; to-day is the sowing, but to-morrow is the harvest; to-day is the battle, but to-morrow is the rest; to-day is the weeping, but to-morrow is the joy; and what is to-day compared to to-morrow? to-day is at most but threescore years and ten, but to-morrow is eternity. Be patient and hope unto the end.

V. The last point is the most important in the text. It is the object on which our eyes are to be fixed: we are to run our race " *looking unto Jesus.*" We are to run, depending on Him for salvation, renouncing all trust in our own poor frail exertions, and counting our own performances no better than filthy rags, and resting wholly and entirely, simply and completely, upon that perfect righteousness which He worked out for us upon the cross. We need not run uncertain of the end, we need not fight in ignorance of what shall follow; we have only to behold the Lamb of God who taketh away the sin of the world, and believe that He hath borne our griefs and carried our sorrows, and will soon present us spotless and unblameable in His Father's sight. And then we are to run, making Jesus our Example, taking no lower pattern than the Son of God Himself, endeavouring to copy His meekness, His humility, His love, His zeal for souls, His self-denial, His purity, His faith, His patience, His prayerfulness, and as we look we shall daily become more like Him. And then we are to run, looking for our blessed Lord's appearing, praying always with all prayer and supplication that He will hasten His coming and kingdom and accomplish the number of His elect. Unto them that look for Him shall He appear the second time without sin unto salvation, and their vile bodies in a moment, in the twinkling of an eye, shall be made like unto His glorious body, and they shall be for ever with their Lord.

Oh, this looking unto Jesus! here is the secret cause which kept that cloud of witnesses steadfast and unmoveable in this narrow way! here is the simple rule for all who wish to enter on the course which lands a man in Paradise! Look not to earth: it is a sinful, perishable place, and they that build upon it shall find their foundation of the earth earthy; they will not stand the fire. Set not your affections upon it, or else you will perish together; the earth shall be burned up, and if you cling to it in death you shall not be divided!

Look not to yourselves! you are by nature wretched

and miserable, and poor and blind and naked; you cannot make atonement for your past transgressions, you cannot wipe out a single page in that long black list, and when the King shall ask you for your wedding-garment you will be speechless. Look simply unto Jesus, and then the weight shall fall from off your shoulders, and the course shall be clear and plain, and you shall run the race which is set before you. Truly a man may be mistaken for a season, and walk in darkness for a time, but if he once determine to look to Jesus he shall not greatly err.

Who now are the men and women in this congregation who have not entered on the grand struggle for life? This day, ye Christless, sleeping ones, this day I charge you to be honest and merciful to your souls. Turn ye, O turn ye from your evil ways, turn ye from your self-pleasing and self-indulging; seek ye the Lord while He may be found, call upon Him while He is near; cry mightily unto the Lord Jesus Christ, before the night cometh and you sleep for evermore. I know the thoughts that are in the hearts of those among you who ever think, (for many come and go without thinking): I know your thoughts; you cannot make up your mind to lay aside every weight, you cannot throw overboard the sin that doth so easily beset you. Alas! like Herod you would do many things, but not all: you will not give up that Herodias, that darling bosom-sin— the world, the business, the drink, the pleasure—you cannot give it up, it must have the first place in your heart. I testify, I warn you, I take you to record, that God hath declared there shall in no wise enter into heaven anything that defileth, and if you are determined not to give up your sins, your sins will cleave to you like lead and sink you in the pit of destruction. You need not wait: you must show some inclination ; God will not convert you against your will ; except you show the desire, how can you expect He will give you the grace ?

But where are the men and women who are running the race and struggling towards the heavenly Jerusalem ? Think not that you have anything which makes your journey more difficult than others' ; the saints at God's right hand were perfected through sufferings ; and you must run with patience ; millions have gone safe through, and so shall you.

Beware of cumbering yourselves with any weight of earthly chances ; examine your hearts most closely, and purge out each besetting sin with a godly prayerful jealousy. Remember that blessed rule, " looking unto Jesus." Peter did run well for a time, when he left the ship to walk upon the sea to Jesus ; but when he saw the waves and the storm he was afraid and began to sink. Thus many a one sets out courageously ; but after a while corruptions rise high within, corruptions are strong without, the eye is drawn off Jesus, the devil gets an advantage, and the soul begins to sink. Oh, keep your eye steadily fixed on Christ, and you shall go through fire and water and they shall not hurt you. Are you tempted ? look unto Jesus. Are you afflicted ? look unto Jesus. Do all speak evil of you ? look unto Jesus. Do you feel cold, dull, backsliding ? look unto Jesus. Never say, " I will heal myself and then look unto Jesus, I will get into a good frame and then take comfort in my Beloved." It is the very delusion of Satan. But whether you are weak or strong, in the valley or on the mount, in sickness or in health, in sorrow or in joy, in going out or in coming in, in youth or in age, in richness or in poverty, in life or in death, let this be your motto and your guide—" LOOKING UNTO JESUS."

Why those fears? behold, 'tis Jesus
  Holds the helm and guides the ship:
Spread the sails, and catch the breezes
  Sent to waft us o'er the deep
      To the regions
Where the mourners cease to weep.

Could we stay when death was hov'ring,
  Could we rest on such a shore?
No, the awful truth discov'ring,
  We could linger there no more;
      We forsake it,
Leaving all we loved before.

Though the shore we hope to land on
  Only by report is known,
Yet we freely all abandon
  Led by that report alone:
      And with Jesus
Through the trackless deep move on.

Render'd safe by *His* protection,
  We shall pass the wat'ry waste;
Trusting to *His* wise direction,
  We shall gain the port at last,
      And with wonder
Think on toils and dangers past.

3.
Ready and waiting

3.
Ready and waiting

"Then shall the kingdom of heaven be likened unto ten virgins, which took their lamps, and went forth to meet the bridegroom. And five of them were wise, and five were foolish. They that were foolish took their lamps, and took no oil with them : but the wise took oil in their vessels with their lamps. While the bridegroom tarried, they all slumbered and slept. And at midnight there was a cry made, Behold, the bridegroom cometh ; go ye out to meet him. Then all those virgins arose, and trimmed their lamps. And the foolish said unto the wise, Give us of your oil; for our lamps are gone out. But the wise answered, saying, Not so ; lest there be not enough for us and you : but go ye rather to them that sell, and buy for yourselves. And while they went to buy, the bridegroom came ; and they that were ready went in with him to the marriage : and the door was shut. Afterward came also the other virgins, saying, Lord, Lord, open to us. But he answered and said, Verily I say unto you, I know you not. Watch therefore, for ye know neither the day nor the hour wherein the Son of man cometh."

Matthew 25:1-13

THIS is one of the most solemn parables that the Lord Jesus ever spoke : partly because of the time at which it was spoken ; partly because of the matter which it contains.

As to the *time*, it was but a few days before our Lord's death. It was spoken within view of Gethsemane and Calvary, the cross and the grave.

As to the *matter*, it stands as a beacon to the Church in all ages. It is a witness against carelessness and slothfulness, against apathy and indifference, and a witness of no uncertain sound. It cries to sinners, "Awake," and it cries to saints "Watch."

Now, I must necessarily pass over many points that might be spoken of in handling this parable. I have no time to follow out many trains of thought which it opens up. I stand here not to make a book, but to preach a single sermon ; and, this being the case, I shall keep to those points which it most concerns you and me to know.

The marriage customs of the country where the parable was spoken *call for a word of explanation.* Marriages generally took place there in the evening. The bridegroom and his friends came in procession to the bride's house after nightfall. The young women who were the bride's friends were assembled at the bride's house to wait for them. As soon as the lamps or torches of the bridegroom's party were seen in the distance, these young women lighted their lamps and went forth to meet him ; then, having formed one united party, they all returned together to the bride's house. As soon as they entered it, the door was shut, and the marriage ceremony took place ; and after that no one was admitted. All these were familiar things to those who heard the Lord Jesus, and it is right and proper that you should understand them.

The figures used in the parable also call for a word of explanation. I give you my own view of their meaning. I may be wrong : but you have a right to know what I think, and I will tell you shortly, but decidedly—I have no time to do more.

I believe the TIME spoken of in this parable means the time when Christ shall return in person to the world. The word "then" compared with the end of the twenty-fourth chapter appears to me to settle the question.

I believe the virgins carrying lamps represent professing Christians, the visible Church of Christ.

I believe the bridegroom represents the Lord Jesus Christ Himself.

I take the wise virgins to be the true believers, the converted part of the visible Church. I take the foolish to be the mere nominal Christians—the unconverted.

I take the oil, which some had and others had not, to be the grace of the Spirit, the unction of the Holy One.

I consider the midnight cry to mean the second coming or advent of Christ into the world.

I consider the going in to the marriage of the wise to mean the reward of the believers. I consider the shutting out of the foolish to mean the final exclusion from heaven of the unbelieving.

And now, without saying anything more of preface, let me go on to point out the great practical lessons which this parable is meant to teach.

I. Learn first that the visible Church of Christ will always be a mixed body till Christ comes again.

II. Learn secondly that this visible church is always in danger of neglecting the doctrine of Christ's second advent.

III. Learn thirdly that whenever Christ does come again, it will be a very sudden event.

IV. Learn fourthly that Christ's second advent will make an immense change to all members of Christ's Church, both good and bad.

Let me try to set each of these truths before you.

I. Learn firstly that the Church of Christ will always be a mixed body till Christ comes again.

I can gather no other meaning from the beginning of the parable. I see wise and foolish virgins mingled in one company—virgins with oil and virgins with no oil all side by side. And I see this state of things going on till the very moment the bridegroom appears. I see all this, and I cannot avoid the conclusion that the visible Church will always be a mixed body till Jesus comes again. Its members will never be all unbelievers; Christ will always have His witnesses. Its members will never be all believers; there will always be imperfection, hypocrisy, and false profession.

I frankly say that I can find no standing ground for the common notion that the Church will gradually advance towards perfection, and that it will become better and better, holier and holier up to the very end. I see no warrant of Scripture for believing that sin will gradually dwindle away in the earth, consume, melt and disappear by inches, like the last snowdrift in spring; nor yet for believing that holiness will gradually increase like the banyan tree, blossom, bloom, and fill the face of the world with fruit.

I have no doubt whatever that true gospel religion admits of ebbs and flows in its progress, of spring tides and of neaps; and that, like the moon, Christ's bride is sometimes full and walking in brightness, and like the same moon is sometimes under an eclipse and scarcely seen at all. That there will always be a vast amount of evil in the world until the second advent, I am fully persuaded. Evil men and seducers shall wax worse and worse, deceiving and being deceived. The tares and the wheat shall grow together till the harvest. I fully expect that the earth will one day be filled with the knowledge of the glory of the Lord, but I believe that day will be in an entirely new dispensation—will not be till after the Lord's return. Till the Bridegroom comes there will always be wise and foolish in the Church.

The wise are those who have that wisdom which the Holy Ghost alone can give. They know their sins, they know Christ, they know how to walk and please God, and they act upon their knowledge. They look on life as a season of preparation for eternity, not as an end but as a way, not as a harbour but a voyage, not as a home but a journey, not as full age but a school. Happy are those who know this !

The foolish are those who are without spiritual knowledge. They neither know God, nor Christ, nor their own hearts, nor sin, nor the world, nor heaven, nor hell, as they ought. There is no folly like soul-folly. To expect wages after no work, or prosperity after no pains, or learning after no diligent reading—all this is folly. But to expect heaven without faith in Christ, or the kingdom of God without being born again, or the crown without the cross—all this is greater folly and yet more common.

Till the Bridegroom comes there will always be some who have grace and some who have not grace in the visible Church. Some will have nothing but the name of Christian, others will have the reality ; some will have the profession of religion, others will have the possession also. Some will be content to belong to the church, others will never be content unless they also belong to Christ. Some will be satisfied if they have only the baptism of water, others will never be satisfied unless they also feel within the baptism of the Spirit. Some will stop short in the form of Christianity, others will never rest unless they have also the substance.

Brethren, the visible Church of Christ is made up of these two classes. There always have been such ; there always will be such until the end. Borderers and undecided ones, whom man's eyes cannot make out, there must needs be. But gracious and graceless, wise and foolish, make up the whole Church of Christ. You are all written down in this parable yourselves.

You are all either wise virgins or foolish virgins ; you
have all oil of grace, or you have none ; you are all
either members of Christ, or not ; you are all either
travelling towards heaven or towards hell.

See now how important it is that we ministers should
divide our congregations in preaching to them. See
how we ought to address you as an assembly in which
some are converted and some unconverted, some are
regenerate and some unregenerate, and some have grace
and some have no grace at all. I know well that
some do not like it ; I know that some fancy that
we should address you all as good Christian people.
I for one will never do so, and I know not how any
one can do it with the Bible in his hands.

There is a notion abroad that all have grace who
have been baptised, and that all congregations of
baptised people should be addressed as regenerate. I
protest against such a notion as a dangerous contradiction of Scripture ; I protest against it as calculated
to confound the minds of people as to what real grace
is. I protest against the idea of grace which nobody
can see, of grace which a man may have in his heart
and yet no one be aware of its existence. I know of
no such grace in Scripture. Grace or no grace, oil or
no oil, living or dead, having the Spirit or not having
the Spirit,—these are the only distinctions that I can
find. These are the old paths, and in them I advise you
to walk. Beware of false prophets ! From ministers
who do not draw a broad line between having the lamp
of profession and having the oil of grace, may the good
Lord ever deliver you !

II. Learn, secondly, that the Church of Christ is
always in danger of neglecting the doctrine of Christ's
second personal advent.

I draw that truth from the solemn words " While

the bridegroom tarried, they all slumbered and slept."
I am quite aware that men explain that verse in
different ways. I stand here to call no man master.
I am set for the proclamation of that which I believe
in my conscience to be true, and I cannot be bound
by the opinion of others.

I do not believe that the words "they all slumbered
and slept" mean the death of all; though many think
so. To my mind such an interpretation involves a
simple untruth. All the professing Church will not be
dead when Christ comes. St. Paul says, "We which
are alive remain (not 'all sleep') unto the coming of
the Lord."

I do not believe that the words mean that all the
professing Church got into a slumbering and sleeping
state of soul, though many think so. Such a view
appears to me to wipe away the distinction between
believers and unbelievers far too much. Sleep is one
of the emblems which the Spirit has chosen to signify
unconversion. "Awake, thou that sleepest," etc.

I believe that the words are to be explained with a
special regard to the great event on which the whole
parable chiefly runs—the second advent of Christ; and
I believe that our Lord's meaning in this verse of the
parable was simply this: that during the interval
between His first and second advent the whole Church,
both believers and unbelievers, would get into a dull
and dim-sighted state of soul about the blessed doctrine
of His own personal return.

And I say deliberately that, so far as my own judgment goes, there never was a saying of our Lord's more
thoroughly verified by the event. I say that, of all
doctrines of the gospel, the one in which we are most
unlike the first Christians in our sense of its true value
is the doctrine of Christ's second advent. In our view

of man's corruption, of justification by faith, of our need
of the sanctifying Spirit, upon these matters I believe
we should find that English Christians were much of
one mind with believers at Corinth, Ephesus, Philippi,
or Rome in olden times; but in our view of the
second advent I believe we should find there was a
mighty difference if we could but compare our experience. We should find that we fell woefully short of
them in our estimate of its importance and realisation
of its nature. We should discover, in one word, that
we slumber and sleep about it.

I must speak my mind on this subject, now that I
am upon it. I do so at the risk of giving offence and
rubbing against prejudices. But speak I must.

I submit, then, that the Church of Christ has gone
too long not seeing that there are two personal advents
of Christ spoken of in the Old Testament—an advent
in humiliation and an advent in glory too, an advent
to suffer and an advent to reign. We have got into
a vicious way of taking all the promises spiritually
and all the curses and denunciations literally. The
curses on Jews and Babylon and Edom and Egypt
we have been content to take literally; the blessings
on Zion, Jerusalem, Jacob, Israel, and so forth, we have
taken spiritually and comfortably applied to the Church
of Christ. No man can read sermons or commentaries
and not be aware of this. I believe it has been a wrong
system of interpreting Scripture. I believe that prophetical denunciations and prophetical promises in their
primary sense are always to be taken literally. That
primary sense we have sadly lost sight of, and by so
doing I think we have got into a slumbering and sleeping
state about the second advent of Christ.

But I say further, that the Church of Christ has
gone on too long putting a strange sense on the passage

which speaks of the coming of the Son of man in the New Testament. Some tell us that this expression always means death. No man can read the thousands of epitaphs on tombstones in which the Son of man's coming is thrust in, and not observe how widespread this view is. Some tell us it means the conversion of the world. Some tell us it means the destruction of Jerusalem. That also is a very common way of interpreting the expression with many. They find Jerusalem everywhere in the New Testament prophecies, and, like Aaron's rod, they make it swallow up everything else. Now, I have no desire to underrate the importance of death, the conversion of the world, or the destruction of Jerusalem; but I must express my own firm belief that the coming of the Son of man is an entirely distinct subject from any of the three I have mentioned. And the acceptance they have met with I hold to be one more proof that in the matter of Christ's second advent the Church has slumbered and slept.

The plain truth of Scripture, I believe, is as follows. When the number of the elect is accomplished, Christ shall come again to this world, with power and great glory. As He came the first time in person, so He shall come the second time in person; as He went away visibly, so He shall return visibly. Then shall be fulfilled those words of Acts i.: "This same Jesus, which is taken up from you into heaven, shall so come in like manner as ye have seen Him go into heaven"; and the words of Zechariah xiv.: "The Lord my God shall come, and all the saints with Thee"; and the words of Enoch in Jude: "Behold, the Lord cometh with ten thousand of His saints." And the grand short-coming of the Church in these days has been and is this: that we ministers do not preach enough about this second advent, and private believers do not think

enough about it. There are a few, but what are they?
Many do not. We none of us live on it, feed on it,
act on it, work from it, take comfort in it, as God
intended us to do. In short, the Bridegroom tarries,
and we all slumber and sleep.

It proves nothing against the true doctrine that
it has sometimes been fearfully abused. I should
like to know what doctrine has not. Salvation by
grace has been made a pretext for licentiousness;
election an excuse for all manner of unclean living;
and justification by faith a warrant for antinomianism.
But if men will draw wrong conclusions we are not
obliged to throw up good principles. We do not give
up the gospel because of the extravagancies of Saltmarsh
and William Huntington, of Jumpers and Shakers;
and we need not give up the second advent because
of the Fifth Monarchy men of the Commonwealth or
Irvingites of our own time.

Nor yet does it prove anything against the doctrine
that it is attended with many difficulties. I do not
think there are half so many difficulties as those
connected with the first coming, and yet those difficulties were all overcome. I am satisfied there are far
more difficulties upon any other system of interpretation,
whatever it may be. And after all, what have we to
do with the " how " and " in what manner" prophecies
are to be fulfilled? Our only question is, " Has
God said a thing?" If He has, no doubt it will be
done.

For myself, I can only give my individual testimony;
but the little I know experimentally of the doctrine
makes me regard it as most practical and precious,
and makes me long to see it more generally received.

I find it a powerful spring to holy living; a motive
for patience, for moderation, for spiritual-mindedness;

a test for employment of time—"would I like my Lord to find me so doing?"

I find it the strongest argument for missionary work. The time is short. The Lord is at hand. The gathering out from all nations of a witnessing people will soon be accomplished, and then the King shall come.

I find it the best answer to infidels. I tell them it proves nothing that all the world is not holy after eighteen hundred years; that it was never said it would be in the present order of things; that the King will come one day and then make all bow before Him.

I find it the best argument with the Jew. If I do not take all the prophecy of Isaiah literally, I know not how I can persuade him that the fifty-third chapter is fulfilled. But if I do, I have a resting-place for my lever which he cannot shake.

Who is there that cannot yet receive the doctrine of Christ's second personal advent? I invite you to consider the subject calmly. Dismiss from your mind traditional interpretation; separate the doctrine from the mistakes and blunders of many who have held it; do not reject the foundations because of the wood, hay and stubble; do not condemn it because of injudicious friends. Only examine the texts which speak of it in the same calm way that you weigh texts in the Romish and Socinian controversy, and I am hopeful as to the result on your mind.

Who is there here that receives the doctrine? Try to realise it more. Alas! how little do we feel it at the very best! Be gentle in argument with those that differ. Remember that a man may be mistaken on this subject and yet be a bright child of God. It is not the slumbering on this subject that ruins souls, but the want of grace. Above all avoid dogmatism and

positiveness, and specially about symbolical prophecy.
It is a sad truth, but a truth never to be forgotten, that
none have injured the doctrine of the second advent
so much as over-zealous friends

III. Learn, thirdly, that whenever Christ does come
again it will be a very sudden event. I draw that from
the verse in the parable : " At midnight there was a
cry made, Behold the Bridegroom cometh, go ye forth
to meet Him."

I do not know when Christ will come. I am no
prophet, though I love the subject of prophecy. I
dislike date-fixing, and I think it has done great harm.
I only assert positively that Christ will come again
one day in person to set up His kingdom, and that
whether the day be near, or whether it be far off, it
will take the Church and world exceedingly by surprise.

It will come on men suddenly. It will break on
the world all at once. It will not have been talked
over, prepared for and looked forward to by everybody.
It will awaken men's minds like a cry of fire at midnight.
It will startle men's hearts like a trumpet blown by
their bedsides in their first sleep. Like Pharaoh and
his host, men will know nothing till the very waters
are upon them. Before they can recover their breath
and know where they are, they shall find that the
Lord is come.

I suspect there is a vague notion floating in men's
minds that the present order of things will not end
quite so suddenly. I suspect men cling to the idea
that there will be a kind of Saturday night in the world
—a time when all will know the Lord's day is near, a
time when all will be able to cleanse their consciences,
look up their best garment, shake off their earthly
business, and prepare to meet the Lord. If any one
here has got such a notion I charge him to give it up

for ever. If anything is clear in unfulfilled prophecy, this one fact seems clear, that the Lord's coming will be sudden, and take men by surprise ; and any view of prophecy which destroys the possibility of its being a sudden event, appears to carry about with it a fatal defect.

Everything which is written in Scripture on this point confirms the truth that Christ's second coming will be sudden. " As a snare shall it come on the face of all them that dwell on the earth," says one place : " As a thief in the night," says another ; " As the lightning," says a third ; " In an hour when no man thinketh," says a fourth ; " At a time when they shall be saying Peace and safety," says a fifth.

Our Lord Jesus Christ Himself uses two most striking comparisons when dwelling on this point. He says in one, that as it was in the days of Lot, so shall it be in the days when the Son of man is revealed. Do you remember how it was ? In the days when Lot went out of Sodom the men of Sodom were eating and drinking, planting and building, marrying and giving in marriage. The sun rose as usual. They thought of nothing but worldly things ; they saw no sign of danger. But all at once the fire of God fell upon them and destroyed them.

He says in another place, " As it was in the days of Noe, so shall it be also in the days of the Son of man." Do you remember how it was in the days of Noah ? Stay a little, and let me remind you.

When the flood came on the earth there was no appearance beforehand of anything so awful being near. The sun rose and set as usual ; the day and night followed each other in regular succession. The grass and trees and crops were growing ; the business of the world was going on ; and though Noah preached con-

tinually and warned men of coming danger, no one
believed him.

But at last one day the rain began and did not cease ;
the waters ran and did not stop. The flood came and
the flood swelled ; the flood went on and covered one
thing after another, and all were drowned who were
not in the ark. Everything in which was the breath
of life perished.

Now, as the flood took the world by surprise, just
so will the coming of the Son of man. It will come
on men like a thunderclap. In the midst of the world's
business, when everything is going on just as usual,
in such an hour as this the Lord Jesus Christ will
return.

See here what solemn thoughts the Lord Jesus Christ's
return should raise in every mind. Think for a moment
how little prepared the world is for such an event.
Look at the towns and cities of the earth, and think
of them. Mark how absorbed are men in the business
of their callings. Banks, shops, law, medicine, commerce,
railways, banquets, balls, theatres,—all and each are
drinking up hearts and souls, and thrusting out the
things of God. Think what a fearful shock would be
the stoppage of all these things,—the sudden stoppage
which will be in the day of Christ's appearing. Yet one
day it shall be.

Look at the rural parishes of such a land as ours,
and think of them. See how the minds of the majority
are buried in farms and allotments, in cattle and corn,
in rent and wages, in digging and sowing, in buying
and selling ; and then fancy the awful effect of a sudden
cessation of all these things,—the final cessation which
must be when Christ comes again to finish all things.
Yet remember one day it shall be. Picture these things
to your mind's eye ; picture your own home, your own

family, your own fireside,—picture, above all, your own
feelings, your own state of mind. And then remember
that this is the end to which the world is hastening ;
this is the way in which the world's affairs will be wound
up. This is an event which might possibly happen in
your own time ; and surely you cannot avoid the conclusion that this second coming of Christ is no mere
curious speculation, but is of vast moment to your soul.

Ah! some will say, I have no doubt : " This is all
mere cant and nonsense. This is all extravagant
fanaticism. Where is the likelihood, where is the
probability of all this ? "

Do not say so. Men said the same in the day of
Noah and Lot ; but they found to their cost that Noah
and Lot were right. Do not say so. The apostle
Peter foretold that men would talk so in the latter
days. Do not fulfil his prophecy by your unbelief.

Where is the cant and fanaticism of that which I
have been saying ? I calmly say the present state of
things will come to an end one day. Will any one
deny that ? Will any one say we are to go on as we
do now for ever ? I calmly say that Christ's coming
will be the ending of the present state of things. I
have said so because the Bible says it. I have calmly
said that Christ's coming will be a sudden event,
whenever it may be, and might possibly be in our own
time. I have said so because thus and thus I find it
written. If you do not like it, I am sorry for it. One
thing only you must remember : you are finding fault
with the Bible, not with me.

IV. Learn, in the last place, that Christ's coming
will make an immense change to all members of
Christ's Church, both good and bad.

I draw that from the concluding portion of the
parable, from the discovery of the foolish virgins that

their lamps were gone out, from their anxious address
to the wise, "Give us of your oil," from their vain
knocking at the door when shut, crying, "Lord, Lord,
open to us," from the happy admission of the wise who
were ready to the marriage supper, in company with
the bridegroom. All these points are food for thought.
But I have no time to dwell on them particularly. I
can only take one single broad view of all. To all
who have been baptised in the name of Christ,—converted or unconverted, believer or unbeliever, holy or
unholy, godly or ungodly, wise or foolish, gracious
or graceless,—to all, the second coming of Christ shall
be an immense change.

It shall be an *immense change to the ungodly*, to
the mere nominal Christian.

They will see the value of real heart-religion if they
never saw it before ;—"Give us of your oil," they will
cry to the godly, " for our lamps are gone out."

Who does not know that spiritual religion never
brings a man the world's praise? It never has done,
and it never does. It entails the world's disapprobation,
the world's persecution, the world's ridicule, the world's
sneers. The world will let a man go to hell quietly,
and never try to stop him. The world will never let a
man go to heaven quietly—they will do all they can
to turn him back. Who has not heard of nicknames in
plenty bestowed on all who faithfully follow Christ ?—
Pietist, Methodist, saint, fanatic, enthusiast, righteous
overmuch, and many more ? Who does not know
the petty family persecution which often goes on in
private society in our own day. Let a young person
go to every ball and theatre and racecourse, and utterly
neglect his soul, and no one interferes ; no one says
" Spare thyself," no one says " Be moderate—remember
your soul." But let him begin to read his Bible and

be diligent in prayers, let him decline worldly amuse-
ment and be particular in his employment of time, let
him seek an evangelical ministry and live as if he had
an immortal soul,—let him do this, and the probability
is all his relations and friends will be up in arms.
"You are going too far," "You need not be so very
good," "You are taking up extreme lines,"—this is the
least that he will hear. Alas that it should be so, but
so it is. These are ancient things. As it was in the
days of Cain and Abel, as it was in the days of Isaac
and Ishmael, even so it is now. They that are born
after the flesh will persecute those that are born after
the Spirit. The cross of Christ will always bring
reproach with it. If a man will become a decided
evangelical Christian he must make up his mind
to lose the world's favours; he must be content to
be thought by many a perfect fool.

But, brethren, all this will be at an end when Christ
returns. The light of that day will show everything
in its true colours; the scales will fall from the poor
worldling's eyes. The value of the soul will flash on
his astonished mind; the utter uselessness of a mere
nominal Christianity will burst upon him like a thunder-
storm. The blessedness of regeneration and faith in
Christ and a holy walk will shine before him like
"Mene, Mene, Tekel, Peres" on the wall. The
veil will fall from his face; he will discover that the
godly have been the wise, and that he has played
the fool exceedingly; and just as Saul wanted Samuel
when it was too late, and Belshazzar sent for Daniel
when the kingdom was departing from him, so will
the ungodly turn to the very men they once mocked
and despised, and cry, "Give us of your oil, for our
lamps have gone out."

But again: the ungodly will seek salvation earnestly

when Christ returns, but not find it. They will find
that opportunities once let slip shall never be regained.
They will seek the oil of grace, they will knock at the
door for admission, they will cry, " Lord, Lord, open to
us," but all in vain.

Who does not know that thousands are urged to
pray now, who never attempt it ? They mean to do so
one day, perhaps ; they fancy it will never be too late
to seek the Lord.

But there is a time coming when prayer shall be
heard no longer. There is a time when the door
by which Saul of Tarsus and Magdalen entered in
shall be shut for ever. There is a time when men
shall know the folly of sin, but, like Judas, too late for
repentance ; when they shall desire to enter into the
promised land, but, like Israel at Kadesh, not be able ;
when they shall see the value of God's favour and
covenant blessing, but like Esau, when they can no
longer procure it ; when they shall believe every jot
and tittle of God's revealed word, but, like the miserable
devils, only to tremble. Yes ! beloved brethren, many
come to this, and many will come to this in the
day of Christ's reappearing. They will ask and not
receive, they will seek and not find, they will knock
and the door shall not be opened to them. Alas,
indeed, that it should be so ! Woe to the man who
puts off seeking his manna till the Lord's day of return !
Like Israel of old, he will find none. Woe to the man
who goes to buy oil when he ought to be burning it !
Like the foolish virgins, he will find himself shut out
from the marriage supper of the Lamb.

But as Christ's coming will be a mighty change to
the ungodly, so also will it be a *mighty change to the
godly*.

They shall be placed in a position of perfect safety.

" The door shall be shut." They shall no longer be vexed by temptations, persecuted by the world, warred against by the devil. Their conflicts shall all be over. Their strife with the flesh shall for ever cease. They shall be where there is no Satan, no world, and no sin. Ah! brethren, the second Eden shall be better far than the first. In the first Eden the door was not shut ; but in the second the Lord shall shut us in.

Furthermore the godly shall be placed in a position of perfect blessedness. They shall go in with the Bridegroom to the marriage ; they shall be with Christ. Faith shall be swallowed up in sight, hope shall become certainty, knowledge shall at length be perfect, prayer shall be turned into praise, desires shall receive their full accomplishment, fears and doubtings shall not rise to mar their comforts, the thought of parting shall not spoil the pleasure of meeting ; the company of saints shall be enjoyed without hurry and distraction, and weariness shall be all unknown. Thus shall they understand the meaning of the text, " In Thy presence is fulness of joy, and at Thy right hand are pleasures for evermore." Then shall they experience the truth of that beautiful hymn which says :

> " Let me be with Thee where Thou art,
>   My Saviour, My eternaI rest;
> Then only shall this longing heart
>   Be fully and for ever blest.
>
> " Let me be with Thee where Thou art,
>   Thy unveiled glory to behold ;
> Then only will this wand'ring heart
>   Cease to be false to Thee and cold.
>
> " Let me be with Thee where Thou art,
>   Where none can die, where none remove,
> Then neither death nor life shall part
>   Me from Thy presence and Thy love."

Is there a single man or woman here that can laugh at true vital religion? Is there any one who persecutes and ridicules true godliness, and talks of people being over-particular and righteous overmuch? Beware what you are doing! Again I say beware. You may live to think differently; you may live to alter your opinion,—but perhaps too late. Ah! there is a day coming when there will be no infidels,—no, not one! "Before the name of Jesus every knee will bow, and every tongue confess that He is Lord." Remember that day, and beware.

Is there any dear child of God here who is mocked and despised for the gospel's sake, and feels as if he stood alone? Take comfort; be patient: wait a little— your turn shall come. When the spies returned from searching Canaan, men talked of stoning Caleb and Joshua. A few days passed away, and all the assembly confessed that they alone had been right. Strive to be like them. Follow the Lord fully, and sooner or later all men shall confess that you did well. Men seem to be afraid of going too far, men seem to be afraid of being too holy. Millions will lament in the day of Christ's return that they had not religion enough; not one will be heard to say that he had too much.

And now, brethren, it only remains for me to close this sermon by *three words of application*, which seem to me to arise naturally out of the parable of which I have been speaking. I heartily pray God to bless them to your souls, and to make them words in season at the beginning of a new year.

1. My first word of application shall be a *question*. I take the parable of the ten virgins in my hands, and I address that question to everybody here present. I ask, "Are you ready?" Remember the words of the Lord Jesus: "they that were ready went in with the

bridegroom to the marriage,"—they that were ready and none else. Now here, in the sight of God, I ask you every one, " Is this your case ? " " Are you ready ? "

I do not ask whether you are a Churchman and make a profession of religion ; I do not ask whether you sit under an evangelical ministry, and like evangelical people, and can talk of evangelical things. All this is the surface of Christianity, and may be easily attained. I want to search your heart more deeply by far. I want to know whether grace is in your heart, and the Holy Ghost. I want to know whether you are ready to meet the Bridegroom, ready for Christ's return. I want to know, if the Lord should come this week, whether you could lift up your head with joy, and say, " This is our God ; we have waited for Him ; let us be glad and rejoice in His salvation."

Ah ! some will be saying, " This is far too high a standard. This is requiring far too much. This is extravagance. This is a hard saying : who can bear it ? " I cannot help it. I believe it is the standard of the Bible ; I believe it is the standard St. Peter sets before us when he tells us to be " looking for and hasting unto the coming of the day of God " ; I believe it is the mark at which every believer should be continually aiming, to be found ready to meet Christ.

I want no man to become a hermit and cease to do his duty in the world ; I call on no one to leave his lawful calling or neglect his earthly affairs. But I do call on every one to live like one who expects Christ to return, to live like a pilgrim and stranger, to live ever looking unto Jesus and leaning on Jesus, to live like a good servant with his loins girded and his lamp burning, to live like one whose treasure is in heaven and best things yet to come, with his heart packed up

and ready to be gone.   Now, is this too much to ask ?
I say decidedly that it is not.

Now, are you ready in this way ?   If not, I would
like' to know what good your religion does you.   A
religion that does not make a man ready for anything
is a religion that may well be looked on with suspicion.
If your religion does not make you ready, its source is
not derived from the Bible.

2. My second word of application shall be an
invitation.   I address it to every one who feels in his
conscience that he has no grace in his heart,—to every
one who feels that the character of the foolish virgin
is his own.   To all such I give an invitation this day :
I invite you to " *awake.*"

You know, many of you, that your hearts are not
right in the sight of God.   In the broadest, fullest sense
you are asleep—not merely asleep about the doctrine
of Christ's second advent, but asleep about everything
that concerns your souls.   You are wide-awake perhaps
about temporal things ; you read the newspapers, it
may be, and have your head stored with earthly wisdom
and useful knowledge.   But you have no heart-felt
sense of sin, no peace and friendship with God, no
experimental acquaintance with Christ, no delight in
the Bible and prayer ; and what is all this but being
asleep?

How long is this to go on ?   When do you mean
to arise and live as if you had a soul ?   When will
you cease to hear as those who hear not ?   When will
you give up running after shadows and seek something
substantial ?   When will you throw up the mockery of
a religion that cannot satisfy, cannot comfort, cannot
sanctify, cannot save, and will not bear a calm examina-
tion ?   When will you give up having a faith which
does not influence your practice—having a book which

you say is God's word, but do not use—having the name of Christian, but knowing nothing of Christ? Oh! when shall it once be?

Why not this very new year? Why not this very night? Why not awake and call upon your God, and resolve that you will sleep no longer? I set before you an open door. I set before you Jesus the Saviour who died for sinners on the cross, Jesus able to save to the uttermost, Jesus willing to receive. Go to Him first and foremost if you would know what step to take. Go to Him in prayer and cry, "Lord, save me or I perish; I am weary of sleeping—I would fain sleep no longer." Oh! "awake thou that sleepest, and arise from the dead, and Christ shall give thee light."

Sun and moon and stars are all witnessing against you; they fill their place in creation, and you do not. Sabbaths and ordinances are witnessing against you: they are all proclaiming there is a God, there is a judgment, and you are living as if there were none. The tears and prayers of godly relations are witnessing against you: others are sorrowfully thinking you have a soul, though you seem to forget it. The very gravestones you walk past this night are witnessing against you; they are silently whispering, "Life is short and death is near," all, all are saying, "Awake! awake! awake!" Oh, brethren, the time past may surely suffice you to have slept. Awake to be wise, awake to be safe, awake to be happy. Awake, and sleep no more.

3. My last word of application shall be an *exhortation* to all who have the oil of grace in their hearts. I draw it from the words of our Lord at the end of the parable. I exhort you to "watch."

I exhort you to watch against everything which might interfere with a readiness for Christ's appearing. Watch against inconsistencies of walk, watch against

besetting sins, watch against the harm of false doctrine,
watch against formality in the use of spiritual things,
watch against slothfulness about the Bible and private
prayer. Backsliding begins from within. Watch
against bitterness and uncharitableness: a little love
weighs more than many gifts. Watch against pride
and self-conceit: Peter said, " Though all men deny
Thee, yet will not I"; and presently fell. Watch
against the sin of Galatia, Ephesus, and Laodicea:
believers may run well for a season, then lose their
first love, and then become lukewarm. Watch against
the sin of Jehu: a man may have great zeal from false
motives. It is a much easier thing to oppose anti-
christ than to follow Christ.

Brethren, believers, let us all watch, and watch more
every year we live.

Let us watch for the *world's sake.* We are the book
they chiefly read ; they watch our ways. Oh ! let
us strive to be plain epistles of Christ.

Let us watch for *our own sakes.* As our walk is,
so will be our peace ; as our conformity to Christ's
mind, so will be our sense of Christ's atoning blood.
If a man will not walk in the full light of the sun,
how can he expect to be warm ?

And, not least, let us watch *for our Lord's sake.*
Let us live as if His honour was concerned in our
behaviour ; let us live as if every slip and fall was a
wound to our Head. Oh ! let us exercise a godly
jealousy for thought, word, and action—motive, manner,
and walk. Never never let us fear being too strict.
" Herein is my Father glorified, that ye bear much
fruit ; so shall ye be my disciples."

4.
The sure hope

4.
The sure hope

"These are they which came out of great tribulation, and have washed their robes, and made them white in the blood of the Lamb. Therefore are they before the throne of God, and serve Him day and night in His temple: and He that sitteth on the throne shall dwell among them. They shall hunger no more, neither thirst any more; neither shall the sun light on them, nor any heat. For the Lamb which is in the midst of the throne shall feed them, and shall lead them unto living fountains of waters: and God shall wipe away all tears from their eyes."   *Revelation 7:14-17*

THIS is a very glorious account, and yet we need not wonder, for it was a vision of heavenly things: you may call it a short glimpse within the veil which separated this world from the world to come. We read in the verses before our text, that the apostle John saw in the spirit a great multitude which no man could number, clothed with white robes, and bearing palms in their hands, standing before the throne and before the Lamb: and not knowing himself who or what these might be, he received information from one of the elders or chief angels, and was told in the words you have heard, that these were the blessed company of all faithful people, the redeemed out of every nation and kindred and tongue, the true children of God, the heirs of everlasting salvation.

I propose this morning to consider fully the account which this elder gave. I counsel you, beloved, to search and see what you know of it in your own selves. The

day shall come when the sun shall become black as
sackcloth of hair, and the moon shall become as blood,
and the stars of heaven shall fall unto the earth, and
they who are strangers to the character described in our
text shall find it had been better for them if they had
never been born. Blessed are they who are not
ashamed to confess that they seek a more abiding city
than this world, even a heavenly one, and count all
things loss if they can only win Christ and be found
in Him.

Now there are three points to be examined in our
text.

I. First, where did these saints come from whom
St. John saw.

II. Second, how they had been able to reach the
place where he saw them.

III. Third and last, what was their reward.

I. First, then, we learn that God's saints have come
out of great tribulation—that is, they have come out
of a world full of sin and danger, a world in which they
have so much to encounter which is hurtful to their
souls that you may truly call it a place of great tribulation. How strange that seems! this earth so fair and
lovely as it appears, so full of everything to make life
enjoyable, this earth on which millions do set all their
affections and have not a thought beyond it, is a
wilderness beset with trials and difficulties to every
true believer. Write this down on the tablet of your
memory, that if you make up your mind to follow
Christ and have your soul saved, you will sooner or
later have to go through great tribulation.

Brethren, why are these things so? Because the
world you live in is a fallen world, the devil is the prince
of it, and by far the greater part of the men and women
on it have shut their eyes and given themselves up to

his service. Once become a follower of Christ, you
will see iniquity abounding on every side, you will see
your blessed Saviour's laws trampled under foot, you
will find the immense majority of those around you to
be spiritually dark, sleeping and dead—some altogether
thoughtless, some resting on a form of godliness without
the power ; and if you love the Lord Jesus in sincerity,
to see your Redeemer thus despised will make the world
a place of tribulation.

But this is not all. The earthly-minded, the thoughtless, will never let you hold on your way in peace. Oh
no ! you are condemning their practices and fashions,
you are a witness against their deadness and neglect of
religion ; and so if you set your face towards Zion they
will try to turn you back. Perhaps it will be laughter,
perhaps it will be hard words ; one day they will accuse
you of pride, another of self-conceit ; sometimes they
will annoy you with arguments, sometimes they will
avoid your company ; but, one way or another, you will
soon discover that the worldly-minded will never let
you go quietly to heaven. You cannot please them.
You may exercise yourself like Paul to have a conscience
void of offence towards all men ; it matters not, you
cannot serve the Lord and Mammon, and if you walk
with God, you will find your way is spoken against by
nearly all.

And then there is your own heart—deceitful, treacherous, and cold—the flesh lusting against the spirit
and the spirit warring with the flesh ; your readiness
to make excuses, your deadness in the use of means,
your wandering thought in prayer, your lack of faith
in sorrow, your presumptuous self-confidence in joy.
O Christian, you have an enemy within which needs
your constant watchfulness ; you have a fountain
of trials in your own breast ; you will have daily

occasion to crucify the flesh with its affections and
lusts. And add to this those cares which you have
in common with all children of Adam—sickness, disease
and pain, the loss of property, the unkindness of friends,
the daily toil for a livelihood, the fear of want, the
many nameless causes of anxiety which every week
almost brings round, and say whether it be not true
that all God's people come out of great tribulation.
They must deny themselves, they must take up the
cross, they must reckon on many a trial, if they would
enter into the kingdom of heaven.

Mark well, beloved, this truth—the path to glory
has been always filled with thorns ; it is the experience
of all those holy men who have left us an example
that we should walk in their steps : Abraham, and
Jacob, and Moses, and David, and Job, and Daniel, there
was not one of them who was not perfected through
sufferings.

We are all too much disposed to think a time may
come when we shall have a season of repose and not
be harassed with these vexations and disappointments.
Almost every one supposes he is tried more than his
neighbours ; but let us not be deceived—this earth is
not our rest ; it is a place for working, not for sleeping.
Here is the reason that so many run well for a time,
and seem to have the love of Christ in their hearts,
and yet, when persecution or affliction ariseth for the
word's sake, they are offended. They had not counted
the cost ; they had reckoned on the reward without
the labour ; they had forgotten this most important
point in the character of God's saints—" they are men
who have come out of great tribulation."

This seems a hard saying, but I would have you
know these trials are laid on us for the most wise and
merciful purposes. We live in such a fair and pleasant

world, we are so surrounded with so much that is smiling and gay, that if we were not often obliged to taste of sickness and trial or disappointments, we should forget our heavenly home, and pitch our tents over against this Sodom. Therefore it is that God's people pass through great tribulations ; therefore it is they are often called upon to suffer the sting of affliction and anxiety, or weep over the grave of those whom they have loved as their own soul. It is their Father's hand which chastens them ; it is thus He weans their affection from things below and fixes them on Himself ; it is thus He trains them for eternity, and cuts the threads one by one which bind their wavering hearts to earth. No doubt such chastening is grievous for the time, but still it brings many a hidden grace to light, and cuts down many a secret seed of evil ; and we shall see those who have suffered most shining among the brightest stars in the assembly of heaven. The purest gold is that which has been longest in the refiner's furnace. The brightest diamond is often that which has required the most grinding and polishing. But our light affliction endureth but for a moment, and it worketh for us a far more exceeding and eternal weight of glory ; the saints are men who have *come out* of great tribulation, they are never left to perish in it ; the last night of weeping will soon be spent, the last wave of trouble will have rolled over us, and then we shall have a peace which passeth all understanding ; we shall be at home for ever with the Lord.

I repeat, this seems at first sight a hard saying ; and yet it is a true one. Count up the enemies which encompass the children of God,—the world with its unkindnesses or its snares and seductions, the flesh with its unceasing backwardness and indifference to the Lord's service, the devil with his arts and devices,—

and see whether you could give a more correct picture
of the saints' experience than may be found in the
words, "these are they which came out of great tribulation." An unconverted man may not understand
this, and a thoughtless man may not consider it; they
neither know nor care about this spiritual conflict;
it is foolishness to them; but they that are born again,
and have learned the value of their own souls, can
set to their seals that it is all true.

II. The second question rising out of the text is
this: "How did these shining ones reach that blessed
place where John saw them?" Think not it was their
own righteousness which brought salvation, and their
own strength which upheld them: the cross will surely
lead to the crown, but the cross will never deserve
it; not all the tears which they have shed, not all the
patience they have shown in tribulation, could ever
avail to make atonement for transgression, or wash
away one single sin. What says the apostle? "They
have washed their robes, and made them white in the
blood of the Lamb." They have not been ashamed
to acknowledge their iniquities, and they have laid
them all before the Lord Jesus Christ, and for His
cross and passion, and for His righteousness' sake they
have sought a free forgiveness, and they have found
it. Lay this to heart, all ye that are wise in your
own eyes and holy in your own sight. No doubt
there were prophets and righteous men of old, men
who had wrought miracles and given their bodies to
be burned, men who had been valiant for the truth
even unto death, in that great multitude which John
beheld; but none came boasting of his own attainments
and clothed in his own apparel,—they were all washed
and made white in the blood of the Lamb.

And lay this well to heart, all ye that are pressed

down with the burden of your sins, if any such there
be, and dare not lift up your eyes to heaven. No
doubt there were sinners before God exceedingly in
that company, many who had been publicans and
harlots, the very filth of the earth and offscouring
of all things, and yet they found a place of forgiveness
and, behold, they are washed, and white as the driven
snow. They were in a world of tribulation like yourselves, but they found time to listen to the report of
God's ministers, and when they listened they believed ;
they did not think scorn of the goodly land before
them ; they did not make light of their Master's
invitations, but they loathed themselves for their past
transgressions and forgetfulness, and with earnest
supplication and prayer sought to the Lamb of God
which taketh away the sins of the world, and no sooner
did they knock than the door was opened. They were
not content with hearing of this fountain for sin and
uncleanness, like many of yourselves, and talking of it
as a thing to be admired, and very useful for others ;
they did not sit beside the pool of Bethesda without
endeavouring to step in, but they cried, " Lord, have
mercy, wash *me*, even *me* also," and so they were washed
they were sanctified, they were justified, in the name of
the Lord Jesus and by the Spirit of our God ; they
obtained a free pardon, and their iniquities were all
taken out of the way. By nature they were as weak
and timid and sinful and shortcoming as any among
yourselves,—there is not a danger or an obstacle or a
doubt or a discouragement in any of your minds with
which they were not familiar,—and yet they were all
saved by the free grace of God, they were washed and
made white in the blood of the Lamb, they were more
than conquerors through Him that loved them. Around
that throne you would find many who used to be the

vilest of the vile. Go up, and ask them, every one,
" How did you come hither? whence got you that white
robe?" They will answer you, " We were once a
generation without God in the world, without light and
without hope, we cared for nothing but fulfilling the
desires of the flesh and the mind, we were known as
drunkards and revilers and fornicators; many a time
we hardened our hearts against advice; many a careless
neighbour did we follow to the grave, and tempted God
to cut us off by continued impenitence; but at last
our conscience spoke so loudly that we dared no longer
delay; we tried to keep God's law, but we could not
answer it one in a thousand, it brought us to flat
despair; we made a great profession, and men said we
were converted; but it would not do—sin lay upon us
like a mountain, all unatoned for, and we were miserable.
But we heard a voice, saying, ' If any man thirst, let him
come unto Me and drink,'—He that believeth on Me,
though he were dead yet shall he live,' ' Come unto
Me and I will give you rest,' and when we heard it,
we went at once to the Lord Jesus Christ, we waited
for nothing, we laid all our sorrows and all our
wickedness before Him, and, behold, that very day we
were healed and made whole, not having spot or
wrinkle or any such thing." Such is the answer you
would get from many in that company which the
apostle saw.

This is the way you must walk in, if you would ever
stand with them in glory. You must lay aside all
pride and self-dependence, you must use the publican's
prayer, you must believe yourself a miserable unde-
serving sinner, you must lay hold on the cross of Christ
with a simple childlike faith, and pray that you may be
washed in His blood and pardoned for His name's sake.
Show me another way of salvation which will bring

you peace at the last ; I cannot find one in the Bible.
I hear of men who live on many a long year without a
thought about this precious washing in Christ's blood,
this precious garment of Christ's righteousness, and yet
can tell us they trust it will be all right with them at
last ; but I never hear that it is right, and if the Bible
be true it is impossible. I see many who profess a
belief in their need of this fountain for sin and uncleanness, but I fear they do no more than talk about it,
they do not count all things loss until they are
forgiven. But whether men will receive the doctrine
or not, the foundation of God standeth sure, and though
the saints of God do form a multitude which none can
number, I cannot read of one who had not washed his
robes and made them white in the blood of the Lamb.

III. The third and last part of my text is that
which describes the reward of the redeemed : " they
are before the throne of God, and serve Him day and
night in His temple : and He that sitteth on the throne
shall dwell among them. They shall hunger no more,
neither thirst any more, neither shall the sun light on
them, nor any heat. For the Lamb which is in the
midst of the throne shall feed them, and shall lead them
unto living fountains of waters, and God shall wipe
away all tears from their eyes." Here is a list of
privileges ; you have heard of tribulation, but it leads,
you see, to comfort ; you have heard of the cross, but
the end is indeed a crown.

Now we can tell you something of the affliction of
God's children, for we are able to speak that we know ;
but when we have to treat of the glory which shall be
revealed, we are on ground which human eye hath not
seen, and we must be careful not to go beyond what
is written.

The saints " shall serve God day and night." There

shall be no weariness in heaven; there shall be no
earthly labours to distract our attention.   Here, alas!
the cares of the world are continually breaking in,
and these poor frail bodies of ours do often tie us
down to the earth by their weakness, even when the
spirit is willing.   We may be on the mount for a short
season sometimes, but our powers are soon exhausted;
but *there* we shall have no wandering thoughts, no
distractions, no bodily wants, we shall never faint.
How little indeed do we worship God in spirit and
in truth; at our very best moments, how cold and dull
we feel towards our blessed Redeemer, how willing to
allow any excuse for shortening our prayers and
diminishing our communion with our Father which is
in heaven; but they that stand before the throne of
God shall feel no fatigue, they will require no repose,
they will count it their highest privilege to be continually singing the song of Moses and the Lamb,
and saying, "Blessing, and honour, and glory, and
power, be unto Him that sitteth on the throne, and
unto the Lamb for ever and ever."

But let us read on.   "He that sitteth on the throne
shall dwell among them."   They shall no longer walk
by faith, and see through a glass darkly, they shall
see face to face the God in whom they have believed,
and behold His countenance as that of a familiar friend.
They shall have no more dark seasons, they shall
never feel that their beloved Lord is at a distance,
they shall never tremble lest they compel Him to
withdraw Himself by their lack of service, but they
shall see Him as He is, and be for ever at His side.
And if, while groaning in their body of sin, the Christian
finds such peace and comfort in drawing nigh to God
in prayer—if even in the flesh he has tasted that
it is a joyful thing to pour out his heart before the

throne of mercy—oh ! who shall describe his blessedness when he shall find himself for ever in his Redeemer's presence, and shall be told, It is finished, thou shalt no more go out ? It is a pleasant thing to have the company of those we love : our very earthly happiness is incomplete while those who have the keys of our affection, the husband, the wife, the brother, the sister, the friends who are as our own souls, are far away ; but there shall be no such incompleteness in heaven ; there we shall have the presence of our glorious Lord before our eyes, who loved us and gave Himself for us, and paid the price of our salvation, even His own blood, and the Scripture shall be fulfilled which saith, " In Thy presence there is fulness of joy, and at Thy right hand there are pleasures for evermore."

But we may not linger here. We read, " They shall hunger no more, neither thirst any more." They shall have no more wants and necessities ; they shall no longer stand in need of daily application for the bread of life, and find their souls starving in the wilderness of this world ; they shall not walk as pilgrims trembling lest their spiritual food should not support them, and thirsting after a fuller draught of the water of life ; but they shall find that prophecy made good, " When I awake up after Thy likeness, I shall be satisfied." But again, " the sun shall not light on them, nor any heat." There shall be no more trial and persecution. There shall not be one reviling tongue nor one ensnaring temptation. The mockers and the flatterers and the scoffers shall be silent for ever, the fiery darts of the wicked will all be quenched ; there will be nothing to mar and disturb the Christian's peace. The time will have come at last when he may rest ; he will be far above the scene of his old conflicts, and the strife shall never be renewed.

But what is the crowning privilege? " The Lamb, which is in the midst of the throne, shall feed them, and shall lead them unto living fountains of water: and God shall wipe away all tears from their eyes." The Lord Jesus Christ Himself shall minister to their comforts; the same kind hand which raised them from the death of sin to the life of righteousness, which healed their spiritual diseases, and brought them health and peace, and made them new creatures upon earth, the same hand shall welcome them in heaven, and conduct them as highly favoured guests to a banquet of happiness, such as eye hath not seen, neither can it enter into the heart of man to conceive. Time was when He sought them out as wandering sheep in the wilderness of this world, and made them members of His little flock by the renewing of the Holy Ghost, and refreshed their weary, heavy laden souls with the water of life. And the same Jesus who began the good work in the days of their tribulation upon earth, the same Good Shepherd shall complete the work in heaven. Here they have tasted something of the streams, a little trembling company, from north and south, east and west, but there they will be gathered round the fountain itself, and there will be one fold and one shepherd, one heart and one mind, and none shall make them afraid. And then there shall be no more weeping, for " God Himself shall wipe away all tears." A dwelling-place in which there shall be no weeping! I know no part of heaven more difficult to imagine. We live in a world of sorrow, a very vale of tears; tears for ourselves and tears for others, tears over our own shortcomings, tears over the unbelief of those we love, tears over disappointed hopes, tears over the graves of those on whom our affections are set, and all because of sin: there would have been no sorrow if Adam had never fallen, but our very weeping is a proof of sin.

Yet it shall not always be so : a day is still to come when sadness shall flee away, and God Himself shall say, Refrain thy voice from weeping, for the former things are passed away. There shall be no sadness in heaven, for there shall be no sin ; the days of our tribulation shall be forgotten ; we shall be able at last to love our God without coldness, to reverence His holiness without torment, to trust Him without despair, to serve Him without weariness, without interruption, without distraction ; the days of weakness and corruption will be past, and we shall be like unto our Lord in holiness as well as happiness, in purity as well as immortality.

And now, beloved, let me ask you what is the purpose for which the Church of God has been established upon earth, and ministers have been appointed to watch for your souls ? What is the object of Bibles and Sacraments, and prayer and preaching ? Is it not simply this, that you may be numbered with the saints in glory everlasting, that you may enjoy those blessings you have heard described ?

Then search and see what solemn questions spring out of my text. Have you taken up the cross ? are you denying yourself ? do you know anything of this spiritual tribulation ? Be very sure except you will declare yourself decidedly on the Lord's side, and fight His battle with the fashion of the world, and the lusts of the flesh, and the wiles of the devil ; you will never stand before the throne in robes of white and carry the palm of victory in your hand.

That carelessness about sin, that trifling with temptation, that earnestness about the things of time, that forgetfulness about eternity, that readiness to swim with the tide about religion, that unwillingness to

become more serious than your neighbours, that fear of
being thought righteous overmuch, that love of the
world's good opinion,—is this what you call coming out
of great tribulation ? Is this sowing to the Spirit ? Is
this striving and labouring after eternal life ? Oh,
look to your foundations, set your house in order. No
empty trust in God's mercy will ever save you. You
were not baptised unto idleness and indifference.
Without a real hatred of sin, and a real forsaking of sin,
Christ can profit you nothing. You never can be made
white with the blood of the Lamb, except you desire
to have this earth's defilements really washed away.

And then consider, lastly, O unhappy children of this
world, could you be happy in the heaven you have heard
described ? Know ye not all, that sickness and death
do seldom work a change of heart, they seldom plant
in man new taste and new desires ?—and do you think
that men who count it a great matter to come to church,
and find the services a weariness and rejoice when
they are over, will such be ready to serve God day
and night in His temple ? Will those who take no
pleasure in drawing nigh to Jesus in prayer, delight to
be for ever in His presence and dwell with Him ? Are
you who never hunger and thirst after righteousness,
are you to be satisfied with the living fountains of water ?
Are you who never know what it is to weep over sin
and corruption, who never grieve over the wickedness
of this world, are you likely to understand the privilege
of that rest when God shall wipe away all tears ? Oh,
no, it cannot be, it cannot be ! Whatever a man sows
he shall also reap ; whatever we love in time we shall
love in eternity ; whatever we think wearisome now
we shall think wearisome then. Ye must be born
again, or heaven itself would be a miserable abode ;
there is no place there for the worldly-minded and

profane. Ye must be renewed in the spirit of your
minds, or ye will hear that dreadful voice, Friend, how
camest thou in hither without a wedding-garment? Ye
must become new creatures; and how long will you
insult your Redeemer by putting it off? Oh! pray
ye to the Lord Jesus Christ, while it is called to-day,
to send His Holy Spirit on you; go to the fountain
while the door of mercy is yet open, wash and be
clean.

But blessed are all ye that mourn, for ye shall be
comforted; blessed are ye that are persecuted for
righteousness' sake, for great is your reward in heaven.
Ye have wept with them that weep, but ye shall soon
rejoice with them that rejoice, and your joy shall no
man take away. It is but a single step, and you shall
be for ever with the Lord, where the wicked cease
from troubling, and the weary are at rest. The worm
may destroy these bodies, and yet in the flesh ye shall
see God, and your own eyes shall behold Him, and your
own ears shall hear Him say, " Come, ye blessed of my
Father, inherit the kingdom prepared for you from the
foundation of the world." The saints whose faith and
patience you have so often admired; the holy men
and women of whom you have so often said, " Oh, that
I were like them "; the ministers who have shown you
the way of life, and implored you to be steadfast and
unmoveable; the friends who advised you to come out
of the world, and took sweet counsel with you about
the kingdom of God; the beloved ones of your own
house, who slept in Jesus and went home before you:
all are there, all waiting to receive you, and there shall
be no more parting, no more weeping, no more separation; and you, even you, this vile body being changed,
shall sing the song of the redeemed: " Unto Him
that loved us, and washed us from our sins in His own

blood, and hath made us kings and priests unto God and His Father, to Him be glory and dominion for ever and ever."

In this world ye may have tribulation, but be of good cheer : your Lord and Saviour hath overcome the world.

5.
Heading for heaven

5.
Heading for heaven

" For I am now ready to be offered, and the time of my departure is at hand. I have fought a good fight, I have finished my course, I have kept the faith: henceforth there is laid up for me a crown of righteousness, which the Lord, the righteous judge, shall give me at that day: and not to me only, but unto all them also that love His appearing."

2 Timothy 4:6-8

IN these words you see the apostle Paul looking three ways,—*downwards, backwards, forward;* downwards to the grave, backwards to his own ministry, forward to that great day, the day of judgment. Let us stand by his side a few minutes, and mark the words he uses. Happy is that soul among us who can look where Paul looked, and then speak as Paul spoke. He looks downwards to the grave, and he does it *without fear.* Hear what he says.

"I am ready to be offered." I am like an animal brought to the place of sacrifice, and bound with cords to the horns of the altar. The wine and oil have been poured on my head. The last ceremonies have been gone through. Every preparation has been made. It only remains to receive the death-blow, and then all is over.

"The time of my departure is at hand." I am like a ship about to unmoor and put to sea. All on board is ready. I only wait to have the moorings cast off that fasten me to the shore, and I shall begin my voyage.

Brethren, these are glorious words to come from the lips of a child of Adam like ourselves. Death is a solemn thing, and never so much so as when we draw near to it ourselves. The grave is a chilling, heart-sickening idea, and it is vain to pretend it is not ; yet here is a mortal man, who can look calmly into the narrow house appointed for all living, and say, while he stands upon the brink, " I see it all, and am not afraid."

Let us listen to him again. He looks *backwards*, to his ministerial life, and he does it without shame. Hear what he says.

" I have fought a good fight." There he speaks as a soldier. I have fought that good battle with the world, the flesh, and the devil, from which so many shrink and draw back.

" I have finished my course." There he speaks as one who has run for a prize. I have run the race marked out for me. I have gone over the ground staked out for me, however rough and steep. I have not turned aside because of difficulties, and have at length reached the goal.

" I have kept the faith." There he speaks as a steward. I have held fast that glorious gospel which was committed to my trust. I have not mingled it with man's traditions, nor spoiled its simplicity by adding my own notions, nor allowed others to adulterate it without withstanding them to the face. As a soldier, a runner, a steward, he seems to say, I am not ashamed.

Brethren, that Christian is happy who, as he quits this world, can leave such testimony behind him. A good conscience will save no man, wash away no sin, lift us not one inch towards heaven. Yet a good conscience will be found a pleasant visitor at our bedsides in a dying hour. Do you remember that place in Pilgrim's

Progress, which describes old Honest's passage over
the river of death? "The river," says Bunyan, "at
that time overflowed its banks in some places; but
Mr. Honest in his lifetime had spoken to one, Good
Conscience, to meet him there, the which he also did,
and lent him his hand, and so helped him over."
Believe me, there is a mine of truth in that passage.

Let us hear the apostle once more. He looks
forward to the great day of reckoning, and he does it
without doubt. Mark his words: "Henceforth there
is laid up for me a crown of righteousness, which
the Lord, the righteous judge, shall give me at that
day: and not to me only, but unto all them also
that love His appearing." A glorious reward, he seems
to say, is ready and laid up in store for me, even that
crown which is only given to the righteous. In the
great day of judgment the Lord shall give this crown
to me, and to all besides me who have loved Him as
an unseen Saviour, and longed to see Him face to
face. My work is over. This one thing now remains
for me to look forward to, and nothing more.

You see, brethren, he speaks without any hesitation
or distrust. He regards the crown as a sure thing,
as his own already. He declares his belief that the
righteous Judge will give it to him, with an unfaltering
confidence. Paul was no stranger to all the circum-
stances and accompaniments of that great day to which
he referred. The great white throne, the assembled
world, the opened books, the revealing of all secrets,
the listening angels, the awful sentence, the eternal
separation, all these were things with which he was
well acquainted. But none of these things moved him.
His faith overleaped them all, and only saw Christ,
his all-prevailing Advocate, and the blood of sprinkling,
and sin washed away. "A crown," says he, "IS laid

up for me. The Lord Himself SHALL give it me."
He speaks as if he saw it all with his own eyes.

Such are the main things which these verses contain.
Of most of them I cannot pretend to speak. I shall
therefore only try to set before you one point in the
passage, and that is the "*assured hope*" with which
the apostle looks forward to his own prospects in the
day of judgment. I shall do this the more readily
because of the great importance which, I feel, attaches
to the subject, and the great neglect with which, I
humbly conceive, it is often treated in this day. But
I shall do it at the same time with fear and trembling.
I feel that I am treading on very delicate ground,
and that it is easy to speak rashly and unscripturally
in this matter. The road between truth and error
is here especially a narrow pass, and if I shall be
enabled to do good to some, without doing harm to
others, I shall be very thankful.

Now, there are just four things which I wish to bring
before you, and it may perhaps clear our way if I name
them to you at once :

I. First, then, I will try to show you that an assured
hope, such as Paul here expresses, is a true and
Scriptural thing.

II. Secondly, I will make this broad concession, that
a man may never arrive at this assured hope, and yet
be saved.

III. Thirdly, I will give you some reasons why an
assured hope is exceedingly to be desired.

IV. Lastly, I will try to point out some causes why
an assured hope is so seldom attained.

I. First, then, I said, an assured hope is a true and
Scriptural thing.

Assurance, such as Paul here expresses, is not a
mere fancy or feeling. It is not the result of high

animal spirits or a lively temperament of body. It is
a positive gift of the Holy Ghost, bestowed without
reference to men's bodily frames or constitutions, and
a gift which every believer in Christ should aim at and
seek after.

The word of God appears to me to teach, that a
believer may arrive at an assured confidence with regard
to his own salvation.

I lay it down deliberately that a true Christian or
converted man may reach that comfortable degree of
faith, that in general he shall feel confident as to the
safety and forgiveness of his own soul, shall seldom
be troubled with doubts, seldom be distracted with
hesitations, seldom be distressed with anxious questionings, seldom be alarmed about his own state ; he may
have many an inward conflict with sin, but he shall
look forward to death, like Paul, without trembling, and
to judgment without dismay.

Such is my account of assurance. Mark it well. I
say neither less nor more.

Now such a statement as this is often disputed and
denied. Many cannot see it at all.

The Church of Rome denounces assurance in the
most unmeasured tones. The Council of Trent declares
roundly that " a believer's assurance of the pardon of
his sin is a vain and ungodly confidence " ; and Cardinal
Bellarmine, their well-known champion, calls it a " prime
error of heretics."

The great majority of the worldly among ourselves
oppose the doctrine of assurance. It offends and
annoys them. They do not like others to feel comfortable and sure, because they never feel so themselves.
That *they* cannot receive it is certainly no marvel.

But there are also some true believers who reject
assurance. They shrink from it as a notion fraught

with danger.   They consider it borders on presumption.
They seem to think it a proper humility to live in a
certain degree of doubt.   This is to be regretted, and
does much harm.

I frankly allow there are some presumptuous fools
who profess to feel a confidence for which they have
no Scripture warrant.   There always are some who
think well of themselves when God thinks ill, just as
there are some who think ill of their own case when
God thinks well.   There always will be such.   There
never yet was a Scriptural truth without abuses,
impositions and counterfeits.   Weeds will grow as
well as wheat in rich ground.   There will be fanatics
as long as the world stands.   But for all this, an assured
hope is a real and true thing.   My answer to all who
deny the existence of real well-grounded assurance is
simply this, " Look at Scripture."   If assurance be not
there I have not another word to say.

But does not Job say, " I KNOW that my Redeemer
liveth, and that He shall stand at the latter day upon
the earth : and though after my skin worms destroy
this body, yet in my flesh shall I see God "
(Job xix. 25, 26)?

Does not David say, " Though I walk through the
valley of the shadow of death, I will fear no evil : for
Thou art with me ; Thy rod and Thy staff they comfort
me " (Psalm xxiii. 4)?

Does not Isaiah say, " Thou wilt keep him in perfect
peace whose mind is stayed on Thee, because he
trusteth in Thee " (Isaiah xxvi. 3)? and again, " The
work of righteousness shall be peace ; and the effect of
righteousness   quietness   and   assurance   for ever "
(xxxii. 17)?

Does not Paul say to the Romans, " The Spirit
beareth witness with our spirit, that we are the children

of God " (Romans viii. 16)? and to the Corinthians,
" We *know* that if our earthly house of this tabernacle
were dissolved we have a building of God "
(2 Cor. v. 1)? and to Timothy, " I know whom I have
believed, and am persuaded that He is able to keep that
which I have committed to Him" (2 Tim. i. 12)?
And does He not speak to the Colossians of the "full
assurance of understanding" (Col. ii. 2), and to the
Hebrews of the "full assurance of faith and of hope"
(Heb. vi. 11, x. 22)?

Does not Peter expressly say, " Give diligence to
make your calling and election sure " (2 Peter i. 10)?

Does not John say, " We *know* that we have passed
from death unto life " (1 John iii. 14)? and " These
things have I written unto you that believe on the
name of the Son of God : that ye may *know* that
ye *have* eternal life " (1 John v. 13), " We know that
we are of God, and the whole world lieth in wickedness "
(1 John v. 19)?

Brethren, I desire to speak with all humility on every
controverted point. I feel that I am only a poor fallible
child of Adam myself. But I must say that in the
passages I have quoted I see something far higher than
the mere " hopes," and " trusts," where so many appear
content to stop. I see the language of persuasion,
confidence, knowledge, nay, I might almost say of
certainty—and I feel for my own part, if I may take
the Scriptures in their plain obvious meaning, assurance
is true.

But my answer furthermore to all who dislike the
doctrine of assurance, as bordering on presumption, is
this. It cannot be presumption to tread in the steps
of Peter and Paul, of John and of Job. They were all
eminently humble and lowly-minded men, if ever any
were, and yet they all speak of their own state with an

assured hope. Surely this should teach us that deep
humility and strong assurance are by no means incompatible, and for this simple reason, if for no other, the
charge of presumption falls to the ground.

My answer furthermore is, that many have attained
to such an assured hope as our text expresses, even in
modern days. Many have appeared to walk in almost
uninterrupted fellowship with the Father and the Son,
have seemed to enjoy an almost unceasing sense of
the light of God's reconciled countenance shining down
upon them, and have left on record their experience.
I could mention well-known names in proof of this,
if time permitted. The thing has been, and is, and
that is enough.

My answer lastly is, it cannot be wrong to *feel* confident in a matter where God speaks unconditionally,
to believe decidedly when God speaks decidedly, to
have a sure persuasion of pardon and peace when one
rests on the word and oath of Him that never changes.
It is an utter mistake to suppose that the believer who
feels assurance is resting on anything he sees in himself. He simply leans on the Scriptures of truth, and
on the Mediator of the new covenant. He believes
the Lord Jesus means what He says, and takes Him
at His word. Assurance is, after all, no more than a
full-grown faith ; a masculine faith that grasps Christ's
promise with both hands ; a faith that argues like the
good centurion, If the Lord speak the word only, I
am healed.

Depend on it, Paul was the last man in the world to
build his assured hope on anything of his own. He,
who wrote himself down chief of sinners, had a deep
sense of his own guilt and corruption, but then he
had a still deeper sense of the length and breadth of
Christ's righteousness. He had a clear view of the

fountain of evil within him, but then he had a still clearer view of that other fountain which removes all uncleanness. He had a lively feeling of his own weakness, but he had a still livelier feeling that Christ's promise, " They shall never perish," would never be broken. He knew, if ever man did, that he was a poor frail bark traversing a stormy ocean. He saw, if any did, the rolling waves and roaring tempest by which he was surrounded ; but then he looked away from self to Jesus, and so had hope. He remembered that anchor within the veil, sure and steadfast. He remembered the word and work and intercession of Him that loved him and gave Himself for him. And this it was that enabled him to say so boldly, " A crown is laid up for me ; the Lord shall give it to me ; the Lord will preserve me ; I shall never be confounded."

II. I pass on to the second thing I spoke of. I said a believer may never arrive at this assured hope, which Paul expresses, and yet be saved.

I grant this most fully. I do not dispute it for a moment. I would not desire to make one contrite heart sad that God has not made sad, or to discourage one fainting child of God, or to leave the impression that you have no part or lot in Christ except you feel assurance. To have saving faith is one thing : to have an assured hope like the apostle Paul's is quite another. I think this ought never to be forgotten.

I know some great and good men have held a different view. I believe that excellent man, Henry, of Weston Favel, the author of *Theron and Aspasia*, was one who did not allow the distinction I have stated. But I desire to call no man master. For my own part, I should think any other view than that I have given, a most uncomfortable gospel to preach, and one very likely to keep men back a long time from the gate of life.

I shrink not from saying, that by grace a man may have sufficient faith to flee to Christ, really to lay hold on Him, really to trust in Him, really to be a child of God, really to be saved ; and yet never, to his last day, be free from much anxiety, doubt, and fear.

" A letter," says old Watson, " may be written, which is not sealed ; so grace may be written in the heart, yet the Spirit may not set the seal of assurance to it."

A child may be born heir to a great fortune, and yet never be aware of his riches,—live childish, die childish, and never know the fulness of his possession. And so also a man may be a babe in Christ's family, think as a babe, speak as a babe, and though saved never enjoy a lively hope, never know the real privilege of his inheritance.

Do not therefore, my brethren, mistake my meaning. Do not do me the injustice to say I told you none were saved except such as could say, like Paul, " I know and I am persuaded, there is a crown laid up for me."

I do not say so. I tell you nothing of the kind. Faith in Christ a man must have. This is the one door. Without faith no man can be saved—that is certain. A man *must* feel his sins and lost estate, *must* come to Christ for salvation, *must* rest his hope on this alone. But if he have only faith to do this, however weak that faith may be, I will engage he will not miss heaven. Yes ! though his faith be no bigger than a grain of mustard-seed, if it only bring him to Christ and enable him to touch the hem of His garment, he shall be saved, saved as surely as the oldest saint in Paradise, saved as completely and eternally as Peter or John or Paul. There are degrees in our sanctification. In justification there are none.

But all this time, I would have you take notice, the poor soul may have no assurance of his acceptance with

God. He may have fear upon fear, and doubt upon doubt, many a question and many an anxiety, many a struggle and many a misgiving, clouds and darkness, storm and tempest to the very end.

I will engage, I repeat, that bare, simple faith in Christ shall save a man, though he never attain to assurance; but I will not engage it shall bring him to heaven with strong and abounding consolations. I will engage it shall land him safe in harbour, but I will not engage he does not reach the shore weather-beaten and tempest-tossed, scarce knowing himself that he is safe.

Brethren, I believe it is of great importance to keep in view this distinction between faith and assurance. It explains things which an inquirer in religion sometimes finds it hard to understand. Faith, let us remember, is the root, and assurance is the flower. Doubtless you can never have the flower without the root; but it is no less certain you may have the root and never have the flower. Faith is that poor trembling woman, who came behind Jesus in the press, and touched the hem of His garment; assurance is Stephen standing calmly in the midst of his murderers, and saying, " I see the heavens opened, and the Son of man standing on the right hand of God." Faith is the penitent thief crying, " Lord, remember me"; assurance is Job, sitting in the dust, covered with sores, and saying, " I know that my Redeemer liveth." Faith is Peter's drowning cry, as he began to sink, " Lord, save me"; assurance is that same Peter declaring before the council in after time, " There is none other name given under heaven whereby we can be saved; we cannot but speak the things we have seen and heard." Faith is the still small voice, " Lord, I believe, help Thou mine un-belief"; assurance is the confident challenge, " Who

shall lay anything to the charge of God's elect? who
is he that condemneth?" Faith is Saul praying in
the house of Judas at Damascus, sorrowful, blind, and
alone; assurance is Paul the aged prisoner looking
calmly into the grave, and saying, "I know whom I
have believed; there is a crown laid up for me."

Faith is life. How great the blessing! Who can
tell the gulf between life and death? Yet life may be
weak, sickly, unhealthy, painful, trying, anxious, worn,
burdensome, joyless, smileless, to the last. Assurance
is more than life. It is health, strength, power, vigour,
activity, energy, manliness, beauty.

Brethren, it is not a question of saved or not saved,
but of privilege or no privilege; it is not a question of
peace or no peace, but of great peace or little peace;
it is not a question between the wanderers of this
world and the school of Christ, it is one that belongs
only to the school, it is between the first form and the
last. He that has faith does well. Happy should I
feel, if I thought you all had it. Blessed, thrice blessed,
are they that believe: they are safe; they are washed;
they are justified; they are beyond the power of hell.
But he that has assurance does far better, sees more,
feels more, knows more, enjoys more, has more days
like those spoken of in Deuteronomy, the days of
heaven upon earth.

III. I pass on to the third thing of which I spoke. I
will give you some reasons why an assured hope is
exceedingly to be desired.

I ask your attention to this point especially. I
heartily wish that assurance was more sought after than
it is. Too many among us begin doubting and go on
doubting, live doubting, die doubting, and go to heaven
in a kind of mist. It would ill become me to speak
slightingly of "hopes" and "trusts," but I fear many

of us sit down content with them and go no further. I would like to see fewer "peradventures" in the Lord's family, and more who could say "I know, and am persuaded." Oh! that you would all covet the best gifts, and not be content with less. You miss the full tide of blessedness the gospel was meant to convey. You keep yourselves in a low and starved condition of soul, while your Lord is saying, "Eat and drink, O beloved, that your joy may be full."

1. Know then, for one thing, that assurance is a thing to be desired, because of the present joy and peace it affords. Doubts and fears have great power to mar the comfort of a true believer. Uncertainty and suspense are bad enough in any condition—in the matter of our health, our property, our families, our affections, our earthly callings—but never so bad as in the affairs of our souls. Now so long as a believer cannot get beyond "I hope and I trust," he manifestly feels a certain degree of uncertainty about his spiritual state. The very words imply as much: he says "I hope" because he dare not say "I know."

Assurance, my brethren, goes far to set a child of God free from this painful kind of bondage, and mightily ministers to comfort. It gives him joy and peace in believing. It makes him patient in tribulation, contented in trial, calm in affliction, unmoved in sorrow, not afraid of evil tidings. It sweetens his bitter cups, it lessens the burden of his crosses, it smooths the rough places on which he travels, it lightens the valley of the shadow of death. It makes him feel as if he had something solid beneath his feet and something firm under his hand, a sure Friend by the way and a sure home in the end. He feels that the great business of life is a settled business—debt, disaster, work, and all other business is by comparison small. Assurance

will help a man to bear poverty and loss, it will teach him
to say, " I know that I have in heaven a better and more
enduring substance.   Silver and gold have I none, but
grace and glory are mine and can never be taken away."
Assurance will support a man in sickness, make all his
bed, smooth his pillow.   It will enable him to say, " If
my earthly house of this tabernacle fail, I have a building of God, an house not made with hands, eternal in
the heaven. . . . I desire to depart and be with Christ.
My flesh and my heart may fail, but God is the strength
of my heart and my portion for ever."

He that has assured hope can sing in prison, like
Paul and Silas at Philippi.   Assurance can give songs
in the night.   He can sleep with the full prospect of
execution on the morrow, like Peter in Herod's dungeon.
Assurance says, " I will lay me down and take my rest,
for thou, Lord, makest me dwell in safety."   He can
rejoice to suffer shame for Christ's sake, as the apostles
did.   Assurance says, " Rejoice and be exceeding glad
—there is a far more exceeding and eternal weight of
glory."   He can meet a violent and painful death without fear, as Stephen did in olden time, and Cranmer,
Ridley, Latimer and Taylor in our own land.   Assurance
says—" Fear not them which kill the body, and after that
have no more they can do.   Lord Jesus, into Thy hand
I commend my spirit."

Ah, brethren, the comfort assurance can give in the
hour of death is a great point, depend upon it, and never
will you think it so great as when your turn comes to
die.   In that awful hour there are few believers who
do not find out the value and privilege of assurance,
whatever they may have thought about it in their lives ;
general hopes and trusts are all very well to live upon,
but when you come to die you will want to be able to
say, " I *know* and I *feel*."   Believe me, Jordan is a cold

stream to cross alone. The last enemy, even death, is a strong foe. When our souls are in departing, there is no cordial like the strong wine of assurance.

There is a beautiful expression in the Prayer-book's Visitation of the Sick. "The Almighty Lord, who is a most strong tower to all them that put their trust in Him, be now and evermore thy defence, and make thee *know* and *feel* that there is none other name under heaven through whom thou mayest receive health and salvation, but only the name of our Lord Jesus Christ." The compilers of that Service showed great wisdom there : they saw that when the eyes grow dim and the heart grows faint, there must be *knowing* and *feeling* what Christ has done for us if there is to be perfect peace.

2. Let me name another thing. Assurance is to be desired, because it tends to make a Christian an active, useful Christian. None, generally speaking, do so much for Christ on earth as those who enjoy the fullest confidence of a free entrance into heaven. That sounds wonderful, I daresay, but it is true.

A believer who lacks an assured hope will spend much of his time in inward searchings of heart about his own state. He will be full of his own doubtings and questionings, his own conflicts and corruptions. In short, you will often find that he is so taken up with this internal warfare that he has little leisure for other things, little time to work for God.

Now a believer who has, like Paul, an assured hope is free from these harassing distractions. He does not vex his soul with doubts about his own pardon and acceptance. He looks at the covenant sealed with blood, at the finished work and never-broken word of his Lord and Saviour, and therefore counts his salvation a *settled thing.* And thus he is able to give an undivided

attention to the Lord's work, and so in the long run to
do more.

Take, for an illustration of this, two English
emigrants, and suppose them set down side by side
in Australia or New Zealand. Give each of them
a piece of land to clear and cultivate. Secure that
land to them by every needful legal instrument, let it
be conveyed as freehold to them and theirs for ever,
let the conveyance be publicly registered, and the
property made sure to them by every deed and security
that man's ingenuity can devise. Suppose, then, that
one of them shall set to work to bring his land into
cultivation, and labour at it day after day without
intermission or cessation. Suppose, in the meanwhile,
that the other shall be continually leaving his work,
and repeatedly going to the public registry to ask
whether the land really is his own—whether there is
not some mistake—whether after all there is not
some flaw in the legal instruments which conveyed it
to him. The one shall never doubt his title, but just
diligently work on ; the other shall never feel sure of
his title, and spend half his time in going to Sydney
or Auckland with needless inquiries about it. Which,
now, of these two men will have made most progress
in a year's time ? Who will have done the most for
his land, got the greatest breadth under tillage, have
the best crops to show ? You all know as well as I
do—I need not supply an answer. There can only be
one reply.

Brethren, so will it be in the matter of our title to
" mansions in the skies." None will do so much for
the Lord who bought them as the believer who sees
that title clear. The joy of the Lord will be that man's
strength. "Restore unto me," says David, "the joy
of Thy salvation ; . . . then will I teach transgressors Thy

ways." Never were there such working Christians as the apostles. They seemed to live to labour: Christ's work was their meat and drink. They counted not their lives dear; they spent and were spent; they laid down health, ease, worldly comfort at the foot of the cross. And one cause of this, I believe, was their assured hope. They were men that said, " We know that we are of God."

3. Let me name another thing. Assurance is to be desired, because it tends to make a Christian a decided Christian. Indecision and doubt about our own state in God's sight is a grievous disease, and the mother of many evils. It often produces a wavering and an unstable walk in following the Lord. Assurance helps to cut many a knot, and to make the path of Christian duty clear and plain. Many, of whom we feel a hope that they are God's children, and have grace, however weak, are continually perplexed with doubts on points of practice. " Should we do such and such a thing ? Shall we give up this family custom ? Ought we to go to that place ? How shall we draw the line about visiting ? What is to be the measure of our dressing and entertainments ? Are we never to dance, never to play at cards, never to attend pleasure parties ? " These are questions which seem to give them constant trouble. And often, very often, the simple root of this perplexity is that they do not feel assured that they themselves are children of God. They have not yet settled the point which side of the gate they are on. They do not know whether they are inside the ark or not.

That a child of God ought to act in a certain decided way they quite feel, but the grand question is, " Are they children of God themselves ? " If they only felt they were so, they would go straightforward and take a decided line ; but not feeling sure about it, their conscience is for ever coming to a dead-lock. The devil whispers, " Perhaps, after all, you are only a hypocrite ; what right have you to take a decided course ? wait till you are really a Christian." And this whisper too often just turns the scale, and leads on to some wretched conformity to the world.

Brethren, I verily believe you have here one reason why so many are inconsistent, unsatisfactory, and half-hearted in their conduct about the world. They feel no assurance that they are Christ's, and so they feel a hesitancy about breaking with the world. They shrink from laying aside all the ways of the old man, because they are not confident they have put on the new. Depend upon it, one secret of halting between two opinions is want of assurance.

4. Let me name one thing more. Assurance is to be desired because it tends to make the holiest Christians.

This, too, sounds wonderful and strange, and yet it is true. It is one of the paradoxes of the Gospel, con-trary, at first sight, to reason and common-sense, and yet it is a fact. Bellarmine was seldom more wide of the truth than when he said, " Assurance tends to care-lessness and sloth." He that is freely forgiven by Christ will always do much for Christ's glory, and he that has the fullest assurance of this forgiveness will ordinarily keep up the closest walk with God. It is a faithful saying in the first Epistle of John, " Every man that hath this hope in him purifieth himself, even as He is pure."

None are so likely to maintain a watchful guard over their heart and life, as those who know the comfort of living in near communion with God. They feel their privilege, and will fear losing it. They will dread falling from their high estate and marring their own comforts by inconsistencies. He that goes a journey and has little money to lose, takes little thought of danger, and cares not how late he travels in a dangerous country. He that carries gold and jewels, on the contrary, will be a cautious traveller: he will look well to his road, his house, and his company, and run no risks. The fixed stars are those that tremble most. The man that most fully enjoys the light of God's reconciled countenance will be a man tremblingly afraid of losing its blessed comfort, and jealously fearful of doing anything to grieve the Holy Ghost.

Beloved brethren, would you have great peace? Would you like to feel the everlasting arms around you, and to hear the voice of Jesus drawing nigh to your soul, and saying, " I am thy salvation "? Would you be useful in your day and generation? Would you be known of all as bold, firm, decided, single-eyed followers of Christ? Would you be eminently spiritually-minded and holy? "Ah!" you will some of you say, "these are the very things we desire: we long for them, we pant after them, but they seem far from us."

Then take my advice this day. Seek an assured hope, like Paul's. Seek to obtain a simple, childlike confidence in God's promises. Seek to be able to say with the apostle, " I know whom I have believed ; I am persuaded that He is mine and I am His."

You have many of you tried the ways and methods, and completely failed. Change your plan. Go upon another tack. Begin with assurance. Lay aside your doubts. Cast aside your faithless backwardness to take the Lord at His word. Come and roll yourself, your soul and your sins upon your gracious Saviour. Begin with simple believing, and all other things shall soon be added to you.

IV. I come to the last thing of which I spoke. I

promised to point out some probable causes why an assured hope is so seldom attained.   I will do so very shortly.

This, brethren, is a very serious question, and ought to raise in us all great searchings of heart.   Few certainly of all the sheep of Christ ever seem to reach this blessed spirit of assurance.   Many, comparatively, believe, but few are persuaded.   Many, comparatively, have saving faith, but few that glorious confidence which shines forth in our text.

Now, why is this so?   Why is a thing which Peter enjoins as a positive duty a thing of which few believers have an experimental knowledge?   Why is an assured hope so rare?

I desire to offer a few suggestions on this point with all humility.   I know that many have never attained assurance, at whose feet I would gladly sit both in earth and heaven.   *Perhaps* the Lord sees something in some men's natural temperament which makes assurance not good for them.   Perhaps to be kept in spiritual health they need to be kept very low.   God only knows.   Still, after every allowance, I fear there are many believers without an assured hope, whose case may too often be explained by causes such as these.

1. One common cause, I suspect, is a defective view of the doctrine of justification.   I am inclined to think that justification and sanctification are in many minds insensibly confused together.   They receive the gospel truth that there must be something done *in us*, as well as something done *for us*, if we are true believers ; and so far they are right.   But then, without being aware of it perhaps, they seem to imbibe the idea, that this justification is in some degree affected by something within themselves.   They do not clearly see that

Christ's work and not their own work, either in whole or in part, either directly or indirectly, alone is the ground of our acceptance with God; that justification is a thing entirely without us, and nothing is needful on our part but simple faith, and that the weakest believer is as fully justified as the strongest. They appear to forget sometimes that we are saved and justified as sinners, and only as sinners, and that we never can attain to anything higher if we live to the age of Methuselah. Redeemed sinners, justified sinners, and renewed sinners doubtless we must be, but sinners, sinners always to the very last. They seem, too, to expect that a believer may some time in his life be in a measure free from corruption, and attain to a kind of inward perfection. And not finding this angelical state of things in their own hearts, they at once conclude there must be something wrong, go mourning all their days, and are oppressed with fears that they have no part or lot in Christ.

My dear brethren, if you or any believing soul here desires assurance and has not got it, go and ask yourself first of all if you are sound in the faith, if your loins are thoroughly girt about with truth and your eyes thoroughly clear in the matter of justification.

2. Another common cause, I am afraid, is slothfulness about growth in grace. I suspect many believers hold dangerous and unscriptural views on this point. Many appear to me to think that, once converted, they have little more to attend to—that a state of salvation is a kind of easy-chair, in which they may just sit still, lie back, and be happy. They seem to fancy that grace is given them that they may enjoy it, and they forget that it is given to be used and employed, like a talent. Such persons lose sight of the many direct injunctions to increase, to grow, to abound more and more, to add

to our faith and the like ; and in this do-little condition
of mind I never marvel that they miss assurance.

Brethren, you must always remember there is an
inseparable connection between assurance and diligence.
"Give diligence," says Peter, "to make your calling
and election sure." "I desire," says Paul, "that every
one of you do show the same diligence to the full
assurance of hope unto the end." "It is the diligent
soul," says the Proverb, "that shall be made fat."
There is much truth in the maxim of the Puritans,
"Faith of adherence comes by hearing, but faith of
assurance comes not without doing."

3. Another common cause is an inconsistent walk in
life. With grief and sorrow I feel constrained to say,
I fear nothing in this day more frequently prevents
men attaining an assured hope than this. Inconsistency of life is utterly destructive of great peace of
heart. The two things are incompatible. They cannot
go together. If you will have your besetting sins, and
cannot make up your minds to give them up, if you
shrink from cutting off the right hand and plucking
out the right eye when required, I will engage you
shall have no assurance. A vacillating walk, a backwardness to take a bold and decided line, a readiness to
conform to the world, a hesitating witness for Christ, a
lingering tone of profession, all these make up a sure
recipe for bringing a blight upon the garden of your
soul. It is vain to suppose you will feel assured and
persuaded of your pardon and peace, unless you count
all God's commandments concerning all things to be
right, and hate every sin whether great or small. One
Achan allowed in the camp of your heart will poison
all your springs of comfort.

I bless God our salvation in no sense depends on our
own works. "By grace are we saved ; " not by works

of righteousness that we have done, through faith, without the deed of the law. But I never would have any believer for a moment forget that our *sense* of salvation depends much on the manner of our living. Inconsistency will dim your eyes and bring clouds between you and the sun. The sun is the same, but you will not be able to see its brightness and enjoy its warmth. It is in the path of well-doing that assurance will come down and meet you. " The secret of the Lord," says David, " is with them that fear Him." " Great peace have they that love thy law : and nothing shall offend them." " To him that ordereth his conversation aright will I show the salvation of God." Paul was a man who exercised himself to have a conscience void of offence toward God and toward man ; he could say boldly, " I have fought a good fight, ... I have kept the faith." I do not wonder that the Lord enabled him to add confidently, " Henceforth there is laid up for me a crown of righteousness, which the Lord, the righteous judge, shall give me at that day."

Brethren, I commend the three points I have just named to your own private consideration. I am sure they are worth thinking over, and I advise every believer present who lacks assurance to do it. And may the Lord give him understanding in this and all things.

And now, brethren, in closing this sermon, let me speak first to those among you who have not yet believed, have not yet come out from the world, chosen the good part and followed Christ. See, then, my dear friends, from this subject the real privilege of a true Christian. Judge not the Lord Jesus Christ by His people. Judge not the comforts of His kingdom by the measure to which many of His subjects attain.

Alas! we are many of us poor creatures. We come short, very short of the blessedness we might enjoy. But depend upon it there are glorious things in the city of our God, which they who have an assured hope taste even in their lifetime. There is bread enough and to spare in our Father's house, though many of us, alas! eat but little of it, and continue weak.

And why should not you enter in and share our privileges? Why should not you come with us and sit down by our side? What can the world give you, after all, which will bear comparison with the hope of the least member of the family of Christ? Verily the weakest child of God has got more durable riches in his hand than the wealthiest man of the world that ever breathed. Oh! but I feel deeply for you in these days, if ever I did. I feel deeply for those whose treasure is all on earth and whose hopes are this side the grave. Yes! when I see old kingdoms and dynasties shaking to the very foundations; when I see property dependent on public confidence melting like snow in spring, when I see stocks and shares and funds losing their value, I do feel deeply for those who have no better portion, no place in a kingdom that cannot be removed.

Take the advice of a minister of Christ. Seek a treasure that cannot be taken from you; seek a city which hath lasting foundations. Do as the apostle Paul did. Give yourself to Christ, and seek an incorruptible crown that fadeth not away. Come to the Lord Jesus Christ as lowly sinners, and He will receive you, pardon you, give you His renewing Spirit, fill you with peace. This shall give you more real comfort than this world has ever done. There is a gulf in your heart which nothing but Christ can fill.

Lastly, let me turn to all believers here present and

speak to them a few words of brotherly counsel. For one thing, resolve this day to seek after an assured hope, if you do not feel you have got it. Believe, me, believe me, it is worth the seeking. If it is good to be sure in earthly things, how much better is it to be sure in heavenly things! Seek to know that you have a title, good and solid and not to be overthrown. Your salvation is a fixed and certain thing. God knows it. Why should not you seek to know it too? Paul never saw the book of life ; and yet Paul says " I know and am persuaded." Go home and pray for an increase of faith. Cultivate that blessed root more, and then by God's blessing you shall have the flower.

For another thing, be not surprised if you do not attain assurance all at once. It is good sometimes to be kept waiting. We do not value things which we get without trouble. Joseph waited long for deliverance from prison, but it came at length. For another thing, be not surprised at occasional doubts after you have got assurance. No morning sun lasts all the day. There is a devil, and a strong devil too, and he will take care you know it. You must not forget you are on earth and not in heaven. Some doubt there always will be. He that never doubts has nothing to lose. He that never fears possesses nothing truly valuable. He that is never jealous knows little of deep love.

And finally do not forget that assurance is a thing that may be lost. Oh! it is a most delicate plant. It needs daily, hourly watching, watering, tending, cherishing. So take care. David lost it. Peter lost it. Each found it again, but not till after bitter tears. Quench not the Spirit; grieve Him not; vex Him not. Drive Him not to a distance by tampering with small bad habits and little sins. Little jarrings make unhappy homes, and petty inconsistencies will bring in a strangeness between you and the Spirit.

Hear the conclusion of the whole matter. The nearest walker with God will generally be kept in the greatest peace. The believer who follows the Lord most fully will ordinarily enjoy the most assured hope.

6.
Home at last!

6.
Home at last!

"There shall in no wise enter into it any thing that defileth, neither whatsoever worketh abomination, or maketh a lie: but they which are written in the Lamb's book of life."   *Revelation 21:27*

BRETHREN, there can be no question about the place described in our text: it is heaven itself, that holy city, the new Jerusalem, which is yet to be revealed.

I would fain begin this my last Sunday among you by speaking of heaven. Before I depart and leave you in the wilderness of this world, I would dwell a little on that Canaan God has promised to them that love Him ; *there* it is the last and best wish of my heart you may all go ; *there* it is my consolation to believe I shall at all events meet some of you again.

Brethren, you all hope to go to heaven yourselves. There is not one of you but wishes to be in happiness after death. But on what are your hopes founded? Heaven is a prepared place ; they that shall dwell there are all of one character, the entrance into it is only by one door. Brethren, remember that. And then, too, I read of two sorts of hope: a good hope and a bad hope ; a true hope and a false hope ; a lively hope and a dead hope ; the hope of the righteous and the hope of the wicked, of the believer and of the hypocrite. I read of some who have hope through grace, a hope that maketh not ashamed, and of others who have no hope and are without God in the world. Brethren, remember that. Surely it were wise and prudent and safe to find out what the Bible tells you on the subject, to discover whether your confidence is indeed well founded ; and to this end I call your attention to the doctrine of my text. There you will find three things :

I. There is mention of the place itself.

II. We are told the character of those who will certainly not be there ; and

III. Who alone will.

The Lord grant you may consider well your own fitness for heaven. There must be a certain meetness for that blessed place in our minds and characters. It is senseless, vain, and absurd to suppose that all shall go there, whatever their lives have been. May God the Holy Ghost incline you to examine yourselves faithfully while you have time, before that great day cometh when the unconverted shall be past all hope and the saints past all fear.

I. First of the place itself. There is such a place as heaven. No truth is more certain in the whole of Scripture than this, there remaineth a rest for the people of God. This earth is not our rest ; it cannot be ; there breathes not man or woman who ever found it so. Go, build your happiness on earth, if you are so disposed ; choose everything you can fancy would make life enjoyable,—take money, house, and lands ; take learning, health, and beauty ; take honour, rank, obedience, troops of friends ; take everything your mind can picture to itself or your eye desire,—take all, and yet I dare to tell you even then you would not find rest. I know well that a few short years, and your heart's confession would be, it is all hollow, empty, and unsatisfying ; it is all weariness and disappointment ; it is all vanity and vexation of spirit. I know well you would feel within a hungering and famine, a leanness and barrenness of soul ; and ready indeed would you be to bear your testimony to the mighty truth, " This earth is not our rest."

O brethren, how faithful is that saying, " If in this life only we have hope, we are indeed most miserable." This life, so full of trouble and sorrow and care, of anxiety and labour and toil ; this life of losses and bereavements, of partings and separations, of mourning and woe, of sickness and pain ; this life of which even Elijah got so tired that he requested he might die ; truly I should be crushed to the very earth with misery, if I felt this life were all. If I thought there was nothing for me beyond the dark, cold, silent, lonely grave, I should indeed say, Better never have been born. Thanks be to God this life is not all. I know and am persuaded there is a glorious rest beyond the tomb ; this earth is only the training-school for eternity, these graves are but the stepping-stone and half-way house to heaven. I feel assured this my poor body shall rise again ; this corruptible shall yet put on incorruption, and this mortal immortality, and be with Christ for ever. Yes, heaven is truth and no lie. I will not doubt it. I am not more certain of my own existence than I am of this, there does remain a rest for the people of God.

And, brethren, what sort of a place shall heaven be ? Before we pass on and consider its inhabitants, let us just pause an instant and think on this. What sort of a place shall heaven be ? Heaven shall be a place of perfect rest and peace. They that dwell *there* have no more conflict with the world, the flesh, and the devil ; their warfare is accomplished, and their fight is fought ; at length they may lay aside the armour of

God, at last they may say to the sword of the Spirit,
Rest and be still.   They watch no longer, for they have
no spiritual enemies to fear; they fast and mortify the
flesh no longer, for they have no vile earthy body to
keep under; they pray no more, for they have no evil
to pray against.   *There* the wicked must cease from
troubling; *there* sin and temptation are for ever shut
out; the gates are better barred than those of Eden,
and the devil shall enter in no more.   O Christian
brethren, rouse ye and take comfort; surely this shall
be indeed a blessed rest.   *There* shall be no need of
means of grace, for we shall have the end to which
they are meant to lead; *there* shall be no need of
sacraments, we shall have the substance they are
appointed to keep in mind; *there* faith shall be
swallowed up in sight, and hope in certainty, and
prayer in praise, and sorrow in joy.   Now is the
school-time, the season of the lesson and the rod, then
will be the eternal holiday.   Now we must endure
hardness and press on faint yet pursuing, then we
shall sit down at ease, for the Canaanite shall be
expelled for ever from the land.   Now we are tossed
upon a stormy sea, then we shall be safe in harbour.
Now we have to plough and sow, there we shall reap
the harvest; now we have the labour, but then the
wages; now we have the battle, but then the victory
and reward.   Now we must needs bear the cross, but
then we shall receive the crown.   Now we are journeying through the wilderness, but then we shall be at
home.   O Christian brethren, well may the Bible
tell you, "Blessed are the dead that die in the Lord,
for they rest from their labour."   Surely you must feel
that witness is true.

But again.   Heaven shall be a place of perfect and
unbroken happiness.   Mark what your Bible tells you

in the very chapter which contains my text, " God
shall wipe away all tears from the eyes of His people ;
and there shall be no more death, neither sorrow, nor
crying, neither shall there be any more pain : for the
former things are passed away." Hear what the prophet
Isaiah says in the twenty-fifth chapter : " The Lord God
will wipe away tears from off all faces ; and the rebuke
of His people shall He take away from off all the
earth. And it shall be said in that day, Lo, this is
our God ; we have waited for Him and He will save
us : this is the Lord ; we have waited for Him, we will
be glad and rejoice in His salvation." Brethren, think
of an eternal habitation in which there is no sorrow.
Who is there here below that is not acquainted with
sorrow ? it came in with thorns and thistles at Adam's
fall, it is the bitter cup that all must drink, it is before
us and behind us, it is on the right hand and the left,
it is mingled with the very air we breathe. Our bodies
are racked with pain, and we have sorrow ; our worldly
goods are taken from us, and we have sorrow ; we are
encompassed with difficulties and troubles, and we
have sorrow ; our friends forsake us and look coldly
on us, and we have sorrow ; we are separated from
those we love, and we have sorrow ; those on whom
our hearts' affections are set go down to the grave and
leave us alone, and we have sorrow. And then, too,
we find our own hearts frail and full of corruption, and
that brings sorrow ; We are persecuted and opposed
for the Gospel's sake, and that brings sorrow ; we see
those who are near and dear to us refusing to walk
with God, and that brings sorrow. Oh, what a
sorrowing, grieving world we live in !

Blessed be God ! there shall be no sorrow in heaven.
There shall not be one single tear shed within the
courts above. There shall be no more disease and

weakness and decay; the coffin, and the funeral, and
the grave, and the dark-black mourning shall be things
unknown. Our faces shall no more be pale and sad;
no more shall we go out from the company of those
we love and be parted asunder—that word, farewell, shall
never be heard again.   There shall be no anxious
thought about to-morrow to mar and spoil our enjoy-
ment, no sharp and cutting words to wound our souls;
our wants will have come to a perpetual end, and all
around us shall be harmony and love. O Christian
brethren, what is our light affliction when compared
to such an eternity as this? shame on us if we murmur
and complain and turn back, with such a heaven before
our eyes! What can this vain and passing world give
us better than this? this is the city of our God Himself,
when He will dwell among us Himself. The glory of
God shall lighten it, and the Lamb is the light thereof.
Truly we may say, as Mephibosheth did to David,
" Let the world take all, forasmuch as our Lord will
come in peace."   Such is the Bible heaven, there is none
other; these sayings are faithful and true, not any of
them shall fail. Surely, brethren it is worth a little
pain, a little labouring, a little toil, if only we may have
the lowest place in the kingdom of God.

II. Let us now pass on and see that great thing
which is revealed in the second part of our text. You
have heard of heaven; but all shall not enter it: and
who are the persons who shall not enter in?

Brethren, this is a sad and painful inquiry, and yet
it is one that must be made. I can do no more than
declare to you Scripture truth: it is not my fault
if it is cutting and gives offence. I must deliver my
Master's message and diminish nothing; the line I have
to draw is not mine, but God's: the blame, if you will
lay it, falls on the Bible not on me. " There shall in

no wise enter into heaven any thing that defileth, neither whatsoever worketh abomination, or maketh a lie." Verily these are solemn words; they ought to make you think.

"Nothing that defileth." This touches the case of all who are defiled with sins of heart, and yet feel it not, and refuse to be made clean. These may be decent persons outwardly, but they are vile and polluted within. These are the worldly-minded. They live to this world only, and they have no thought of anything beyond it. The care of this world, the money, the politics of this world, the business of this world, the pleasures of this world, these things swallow up their whole attention and as for St. James' advice to keep ourselves unspotted from the world, they know not what it means.

These are the men who set their affections on earthly things ; they have each their idol in the chamber of their imagination, and they worship and serve it more than God. These are the proud and self-righteous, the self-honouring and the self-conceited ; they love the praise of men, they like the good opinion of this world, and as for the glorious Lord who made them, His honour, His glory, His house, His word, His service—these are all things which in their judgment must go down, and take the second place. These know not what sorrow for sin means. They are strangers to spiritual anxiety ; they are self-satisfied and content with their condition, and if you attempt to stir them up to zeal and repentance it is more than probable they are offended. Brethren, you know well there are such people ; they are not uncommon ; they may be honour-able in the eyes of men, they may be wise and knowing in this generation, admirable men of business, they may be first and foremost in their respective callings,

but still there is but one account of them ; they bring
no glory to their Maker, they are lovers of themselves
more than of God, and therefore they are counted as
defiled in His sight and nothing that is defiled shall
enter heaven.

But again : " Nothing that worketh abomination."
This touches the case of all who practise those sins of
life which God has pronounced abominable, and take
pleasure in them, and countenance those who practise
them. These are the men who work the works of the
flesh, each as his heart inclines him. These are the
adulterers, fornicators, and unclean livers ; these are
the drunkards, revellers, and gluttons ; these are the
blasphemers, swearers, and liars. These are the men
who count it no shame to live in hatred, variance,
wrath, strife, envyings, quarrellings and the like. They
throw the reins on the neck of their lusts ; they follow
their passions wherever they may lead them ; their
only object is to please themselves.

Brethren, you know well there are such people. The
world may give smooth names to their conduct, the world
may talk of them as light and gay, and loose and wild,
but it will not do. They are all abominable in the
sight of God, and except they be converted and born
again, they shall in no wise enter heaven.

Once more : " Nothing that maketh a lie." This
touches the case of hypocrites. These are the false
professors ; the lip-servants ; they say that they know
God, but in works they deny Him ; they are like barren
fig-trees, all leaves and no fruit ; they are like tinkling
cymbals, all sound, but hollow, empty and without
substance ; these have a name to live while they are
dead, and a form of godliness without the power.
They profess what they do not practise, they speak
what they do not think, they say much and do little,

their words are most amazing, their actions are most poor. These men can talk most bravely of themselves ; no better Christians than they are, if you will take them at their own valuation. They can talk to you of grace, and yet they show none of it in their lives ; they can talk to you of saving faith, and yet they possess not that charity which is faith's companion. They can declaim against forms most strongly, and yet their own Christianity is a form and no more ; they can cry out loudly against Pharisees, and yet no greater Pharisees than they are themselves.

Oh, no ; this religion is of a sort that is public, and not private ; plenty abroad, but none at home ; plenty without, but none within ; plenty in the tongue, but none in the heart. They are altogether unprofitable, good for nothing, they bear no fruit.

Brethren, you must know well there are such miserable persons ; alas ! the world is full of them in these latter days. They may deceive ministers, they may deceive their neighbours, they may even deceive their friends and family, they may try hard to deceive themselves ; but they are no better than liars in God's sight, and except they repent, they shall in no wise enter heaven.

Brethren, consider well these things : " the sin-defiled, the abominable, the hypocrite, shall in no wise enter into heaven." Look well to your own souls ; judge yourselves that ye be not judged of the Lord ; I call heaven and earth to witness this day, they that will live these bad lives, whether they be Churchmen or dissenters, old or young, rich or poor, *they shall* in no wise enter in. Go, cleave to the ways of the world if you are so determined, stick to your sins if you must needs keep them, but I warn you solemnly this hour, they that will have these things shall in no wise enter

in. Go, blame me now for speaking sharply to you—
think I am too particular if you like it—but, oh!
remember if you ever stand without the gates, crying,
" Lord, open to us," in vain, remember there was a time
when I told you, the worldly-minded and the evil livers
shall in no wise enter in. Brethren, I have told you
before, and I tell you now again for the last time, if
you will cling to the things that God hates, you shall
in no wise enter into heaven.

III. Brethren, we must pass on. The text has told
you who shall not enter heaven. Oh! what a mighty
crowd those words shut out! But it tells you something
more: who are they that shall. Short is the account and
simple: " They only that are written in the Lamb's
book of life." What is this book of life? There is a
book, a little book, a book prepared from all eternity,
which God the Father keeps sealed—the book of His
election ; of that book man knows nothing, excepting
this blessed truth that there is such a book. With that
book man has little or nothing to do. But there is
another book, a little book, a book belonging specially
to the Lord Jesus Christ, a book still unfinished, though
year after year there are more names written in it ; a
book still open, still ready to receive the names of
believing penitents : there are still some blank pages left
for you ; and this is the Lamb's book of life. And who
are written in this precious book? I do not know their
names, but I do know their characters, and what those
characters are I will endeavour to tell you shortly, for
the last time.

They are all true penitents. They have been con-
vinced of their own unworthiness in God's sight ; they
have felt themselves to be sinners in deed and in truth ;
they have mourned over their sins, hated their sins,
forsaken their sins ; the remembrance of them is grievous,

the burden of them intolerable ; they have ceased to think well of their own condition and count themselves fit to be saved ; they have confessed with their whole heart : " Lord, we are really chief of sinners—Lord, we are indeed unclean."

Again : they are all believers in Christ Jesus. They have found out the excellency of the work He did to save them, and cast on Him the burden of their souls. They have taken Christ for their all in all : their wisdom, their righteousness, their justification, their forgiveness, their redemption. Other payment of their spiritual debts they have seen none ; other deliverances from the devil they have not been able to find. But they have believed on Christ, and come to Christ for salvation ; they are confident that what they cannot do Christ can do for them, and having Jesus Christ to lean on, they feel perfect peace.

Once more : they are all born of the Spirit and sanctified. They have all put off the old man with his deeds, and put on the new man which is after God. They have all been renewed in the spirit of their minds; a new heart and a new nature has been given to them. They have brought forth those fruits which only are the proof of the Spirit being in them. They may have slipped and come short in many things ; they may have mourned over their own deficiencies full often ; but still, the general bent and bias of their lives has always been towards holiness,—more holiness, more holiness, has always been their hearts' desire. They love God, and they must live to Him. Such is the character of them that are written in heaven. These, then, are the men whose names are to be found in the Lamb's book of life.

Once they may have been as bad as the very worst— defiled, abominable, liars : what matter ? they have re- pented and believed, and now they are written in the

book of life. They may have been despised and rejected
of this world, poor and mean and lowly in the judgment
of their neighbours : what matter ? they had repentance
and faith and new hearts, and now they are written
in the glorious book of life. They may have been of
different ranks and nations ; they may have lived at
different ages, and never seen each other's faces : what
matter ? they have one thing at least in common, they
have repented and believed, and been born again, and
therefore they stand all together in the Lamb's book
of life.

Yes, brethren, these are the men and women that
enter heaven ; nothing can keep them out. Tell me
not of deathbed evidences, and visions and dreams of
dying people ; there is no evidence like that of Christ's
followers—repentance, faith, and holiness ; this is a
character against which the gates shall never be closed.
Repent and believe in Christ and be converted, and
then, whatever happens to others, you, at least, shall
enter heaven ; you shall in no wise be cast out.

And now, men and brethren, in conclusion, let me
press upon you my old question. How is it with yourselves ? What, no answer ! Are you ready to depart ?
Again, no answer ! Is your name written in the book
of life ? Once more, have you no answer?

Oh, think, think, unhappy man or woman, whoever
thou art, think what a miserable thing it is to be
uncertain about eternity. And then consider, if thou
canst not give thy heart to God now, how is it possible
thou couldest enjoy God's heaven hereafter? Heaven
is unceasing godliness ; it is to be in the presence of
God and His Christ for evermore. God is the light,
the food, the air of heaven. It is an eternal sabbath.
To serve God is heaven's employment, to talk with
God is heaven's occupation.

O sinners, sinners, could ye be happy there ? to which of all the saints would ye join yourselves, by whose side would ye go and sit down, with whom of all the prophets and apostles would ye love to converse ? Surely it would be a wearisome thing to you ; surely you would soon want to go forth and join your friends outside. Oh, turn ye, turn ye while it is called to-day ! God will not alter heaven merely to please you ; better a thousand times to conform to His ways while ye can. Ye must love the things of heaven before your death, or else ye cannot enter heaven when ye die.

Christian, look up and take comfort. Jesus has prepared a place for you, and they that follow Him shall never perish, neither shall any man pluck them out of His hands. Look forward to that glorious abode He has provided ; look forward in faith, for it is thine. O Christian brethren, think what a glorious meeting that shall be. There we shall see the saints of old, of whom we have so often read ; there we shall see those holy ministers whose faith and patience we have admired ; there we shall see one another round the throne of our common Saviour, and be parted and separated no more. There we shall labour and toil no more, for the days of mourning shall be ended. Oh, but my heart will leap within me, if I see there faces I have known among you ; if I hear the names of any of yourselves ! The Lord grant it, the Lord bring it to pass. The Lord grant we may some of us, at least, come together in that day, when there shall be one fold and one Shepherd, and with one heart and voice join that glorious song, "Worthy is the Lamb that was slain ; blessing and honour and glory and power be unto the Lamb for ever and ever."